Nulla Nulla

A Collection of Australian Prose & Poems

By
Cecil Roy Mackaway

NULLA NULLA

By Australian Author
Cecil Roy Mackaway

Published by Jan Hawkins
Copyright 2013 Jan Hawkins
ISBN 978-0-9872896-4-3(pbk)

> National Library of Australia Cataloguing-in-Publication entry
> Author: Mackaway, Cecil R.
> Title: Nulla Nulla : a breath of yesteryear / Cecil R. Mackaway
>   sketch artist, Eric Hawkins.
> ISBN: 9780987289643 (pbk.)
> Series: Around the campfire series ; 7.
> Notes: Includes index.
> Subjects: Mackaway, Cecil R.
>   Country life--Australia.
>   Australia--History.

A NOTE FROM THE PUBLISHER

The Author gave the copyright to this collection of prose and poems into my care some years ago, to be published in time. I found the writing so delightful and entertaining that I have published it now for the general public. I invite you to step back into colonial Australia, into a time now passed and see the world through the eyes of someone who enjoyed the adventure of life and the living of it.

These works have been presented as originally written with minimal editing, preserving the vernacular and prose of the era passed where possible, which may be seen in the use of *italic's*. The terms used in the past may not be appropriate if used in the discourse of the present day. If these terms are likely to offend, please do not read this book. Neither the Author nor Publisher intends to offend.

In publishing these works I would like to introduce Cecil Roy Mackaway, a friend, a relative and an inspiring writer and poet.

Jan Hawkins

A Collection of Australian Prose & Poems

FROM THE MEMOIRS OF CECIL ROY MACKAWAY	**5**
STATION LIFE IN OUTBACK	7
PUB LIFE ON THE GOLDFIELDS	14
LIVING IN THE BUSH AT KRAMBACH	17
GROWING UP WITH GRAN	21
HORSES AND HELP	25
OLE WORLD DISCIPLINE	30
THE FAIRER SEX	35
THE GHOST OF GOANNA GULLY	39
IN THE GOOD OLE' DAYS	42
THE DREADED PICKLE POULTICE	46
THE HOT CAT	47
A FLIGHT, WITH BLUE HEALER POWER	49
THE BUSH CAMP	51
FLYING HIGH	56
THE BIG FISHING BUSINESS	58
THE I'S GET IT	64
A NOTE FROM THE AUTHOR CECIL ROY MACKAWAY	**73**

Copyright held by: Jan Hawkins (2013)
Author: Cecil Roy Mackaway
Photographer: Jan Hawkins
Sketch Drawings: Eric S. Hawkins

A BREATH OF YESTERYEAR

FROM THE MEMOIRS OF CECIL ROY MACKAWAY

I was born in 1912 and reared at Dyers Crossing on the Wallamba River in New South Wales, Australia. My Grandmother was the daughter of a young Englishman, he was sent out to the colonies by his family for colonial experience like so many young men from England. It is believed however that he was murdered on the gold fields at Bendigo.

My Grandmothers Stepfather, Mr Rolf, was a *jack-of-all-trades*. In his time he took to droving, station managing, fencing and dam sinking. He travelled a lot by horse and bullock dray, taking his family along with a couple of goats and some fowls when conditions were suitable.

At one time when my grandmother only had two sisters, her father and a mate had a contract to drove a mob of cattle from Wagga Wagga to Rockhampton in Queensland, some 1,000 miles (1560klm), but after about four days on the track the mate was thrown off his horse and killed. They had with them also a *black boy* who drove the horses and dray.

Grandmother's father had to ride back to Wagga to report the death and bring back a policeman who could make the report and help bury the man. So he put the man under the dray and then they covered the whole with a big tarpaulin. Gran, her mother and sisters slept in the dray that night, however early in the morning her mother heard slight noises outside, so she slipped the children and herself between the tarpaulin and cart and they all got underneath with the dead man.

The *black boy*; he had gone bush in a hurry and in the panic under the cart Gran bumped her skull on the axel of the cart. To stop her from yelling her mother clapped her hand over her kisser and almost suffocated her.

One of those *jackey's* who was creating all this strife put his hand up under the tarpaulin to feel if there was anything he could lift. Well he touched the stiff's cold foot and next he give one awful hell of a scream, which sent all the wombats underground for miles. The mob went bush in a hell of a hurry.

Two days later when her father and the copper arrived, the stink of the corps was beginning to attract the crows from *'halfway to Bourke'*. The trooper looked at the tracks and said that there could have been up to a couple of dozen of the *'sunburned jokers'* sniffing around, but they smelt the stiff, and when they touched his cold foot it really was getting too close to the bedevilled.

So the poor stiff had done a good job, even after he had gone to the great cattle drive in the skies. The *copper* said, but only for the dead man they would have been murdered for sure as these *jackey's* had speared a stockman a few days before.

The dead man was buried and the two police helped her father and his new man muster the cattle again. So they went off on their merry way on to Rockhampton with no more mishaps. They only lost about thirty head of cattle out of the three hundred. Not a bad job, as to say, as there were no roads in those days and the blacks were giving them the silent message by smoke to get out of their territory.

At another time when they were on a station, all the men were out mustering when a well-dressed man rode up. His horse was all in a-lather of sweat and he rode up to Gran's mother and asked her for a meal of which she obliged. After he had offered her a sovereign in payment, of which she refused, he then turned to Gran who was only a child and said.

"Here little girl, buy yourself a nice little dress." Then he asked, *"Where is the best horse on the station?"*

By now Gran's mother woke up to who he was.

"Yes," he said. *"I am Thunderbolt, and the police are not far behind me."*

So he took a purebred from the stable, he was a very valuable stallion, and he said, "I will return him later."

True to his world they found the stallion one morning some time later, back in his stable and in perfect condition.

OLD COBBERS

I sit alone in my mountain home with a pencil in my hand,
tryin' to think of a line or two, for my cobbers down on the Strand.
They're rushing here and rushing there as if life is just one way,
and they forget their mates up bush, that they knew in another day.

So life goes on and years pass by, where's it getting you in the end?
A cripple from the rush and strife, or slightly 'round the bend.
So I'll sit up here and write good cheer for them mates down on the Strand,
and tell them about the fish I caught and the latest about the brand.

Perhaps they will think of me while strolling in the Strand.

STATION LIFE IN OUTBACK

There used to be *croc's* in the river at Rockhampton in those days. I remember Gran saying how her an' a little *black girl* with a little dog were playing near the river one day when a big *croc'* came out after the dog. Gran and the little girl got away but the little kelpie pup made him a nice juicy mouthful.

There was another time on a station when the men were once more away mustering and the *blacks* raided the station, which was around a hundred miles away. They killed a mother, Grandmother and four children. The eldest son was out with the men and his father and when they arrived home and discovered the results of the raid they went with two other men on a shooting rampage an' they shot every *black* in sight.

Now their boss had reared a *black boy* from a piccaninny, he was fourteen and when they rode up he ran and hid under the boss's bed. After all the protesting that the boss made they still found him and that was where he was shot, under the bed. A letter was sent to the Governor about it and another to England until all the slaughter was stopped.

Gran's father had been able to talk some *black lingo*. He was always having some of the old men around the station teaching him the *black* language and it saved his life on two occasions while he was out mustering and riding. Twice he was surrounded but after talking to them and then shooting them a beast to take, he managed to get out of trouble.

Gran's father always treated the *blacks* with respect and was well rewarded for his respect. On one occasion when Gran was very young, she followed a pet lamb away from the station. For three days they searched in the Queensland heat until all the station hands had given up. All, to a man said she would be dead but her mother asked the station *gins* if they would look for her. They were just as *good a tracker* as most of the men and in return she promised a red frock to each of them if they found her.

They took a pillow to carry her home, they knew if they found her she would be sore from sunburn and it would hurt her a great deal, so much so that she would not have a chance of living.

About eleven o'clock on the fourth day, an old man pointed out smoke signals in the very distant and her mother asked what they said.

"Black fellow smoke say missus they have found her, she still alive five mile out from the sand-hill," was her answer.

Gran had stripped herself and was curled up around the butt of a small bush to die; she was bitten and blind. The men raced out on horses and her father carried her home on a pillow in the front of him, up on the pommel of his saddle.

After several days when she was soaked in olive oil and given a few drops of brandy and goat milk at every hour, she recovered. But her eyes were so badly eaten by the ants. It took several months and much more care before she could see again.

It also took her mother many weeks and many yards of red flannel to keep her promise. The men got two sticks of tobacco each and they roasted a bullock for all.

At another time the boss was entertaining some visitors and in them days the kitchen was always some distance from the house and it also contained the big bread ovens. The Chinese cook was a very good one and most homestead's kept several milking goats. So they also kept a very mean savage billy who would hit you in the stern at every given chance.

On this occasion the cook was carrying some hard earned hours of flash cooking over to the house for the *'toffs.'* It was all sitting pretty on a nice silver tray but the billy, with no respect, lined the cook up from astern and charged. The poor cook landed on his face amid all the jellies and custards and so on. Billy was found some month's later half eaten by the ants, he had his throat cut.

They were never short of ducks or fish on the station and they had a young *black* who was a champion hunter. A mallee hen, emu's eggs and kangaroo tail soup was always in good supply.

This hunter's favourite sport was catching ducks. He would drift out up beside a duck, grab it by the legs with one hand and pull him under. Then he would change the duck over to the other hand until he had several in his other hand, drowned and silent. It usually took time for the other ducks to wake up that their mates were disappearing.

This same boy had a fight over a *young gin* and he was speared in the thigh. However, he would not let anyone treat him. Only his dog who kept the wound clean by licking it for two weeks. The *station blacks* fed him and after about six months he went walk-about again and bought back his little sweet heart. There was a big corroboree at the camp that night and she also got a red flannel dress. In return for this she gave Gran a little basket made from some kind of hard beans and kangaroo sinew.

Gran kept it for many years and the sinew was later replaced by another *gin*, with hat wire, this when the kangaroo sinew started to rot away.

One day when Gran was about twelve and the men were away mustering, a wild tribe surrounded the house demanding tucker. The *house blacks* had rushed into the house when they had seen them coming and had barred all the doors and shutters. Gran's mother then pushed a sheet of bark aside, from which the fireplace wall was made and handed out some meat and a few loaves of homemade bread.

They were lucky, the tribe then decided to move fast and the men got home about half an hour later. It is believed that the tribe had a scout who had given them the alarm.

Gran's parents, her four stepsisters, two brothers and herself then decided to come back to settle down at Temora in New South Wales. But one of the brothers died when still a boy, on the way back. His last request was for a piece of steak from the best that they had killed that day. He died that night. There is a lonely grave, forgotten somewhere on the way back between Rockhampton and Temora. It is my Gran's little brother.

Gran recalls her mother saying that while they were on the Bendigo diggings, she seen long benches about twenty foot long, these having a quart pot of gold nuggets. Some of these were as big as her thumb, all of them lined up for the Chinese to start gambling for the night. Her mother and the lady in the next tent would wash all the tailings for the small pieces of gold. The men were only interested in pieces pea size or bigger.

One day two bullock drays of supplies landed at the tent store and among the goodies were the first sardines that they had ever seen. Gran's mother paid five pounds for a tin. For all those years when I was a boy living with Gran, her favourite snack was sardines and Sao biscuits', same here for me.

The young goats on the gold fields had a favourite sport, on a winter morning when the tents were covered with frost they would walk up the wide side poles and then come sliding down. I reckon it would be a bit rough on the tents but anyways; it would be a good alarm clock.

There were goats in the hundreds for milking and eating. A little bread was enough to bring them back to camp each evening. Once Gran's mother got one pound for rearing a purebred baby ram on goat milk for the local sheep station. They reckoned that by this way it made a better working ram.

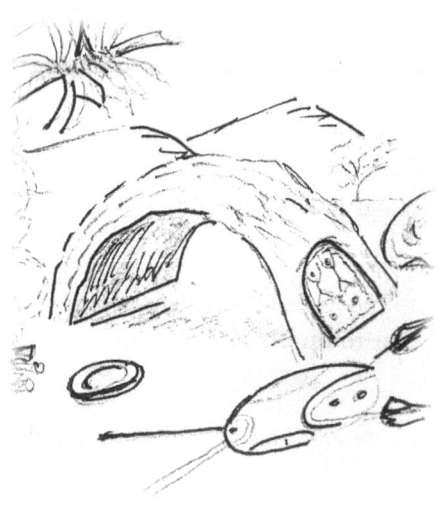

On one station Gran had a pet galah who would run loose around the house. Once the Boss was having dinner with them and he tossed his new cabbage-tree hat down on a stool while they were having dinner. Cocky got busy and he cropped the rim clean off the headpiece. The boss wasn't too happy about that advent.

She also had a pet emu named Ned and for many years his favourite sport was to wait out for any horse that would be tied to the garden fence, this is where visitors would normally tie their horses. Ned would wait and then walk up an' give the horses a pick on the nose. Needless to say, a broken bridle and a bolting horse would arrive back to the station from where it came, without the rider.

Another bit of fun for Ned was to go into the killing yard and run away with the knives, if he could spot one that was handy. One day a young jackeroo threw a lasso around his neck as he was getting away with a knife, it broke his neck. The poor jackeroo tried for months after to make friends with Gran but it was no-go. He even bought her a kelpie pup and another time a new hat from Wagga to help her forget the emu. Gran would tell me some of the stories of her childhood and they were wonderful to listen to.

About Grandad, I don't know much about his young life. He came to Australia at eleven years of age, from Kent in England, with his parents. They settled down at Mamey Johnsons Creek near Stroud where he lived till he was a young man. He learnt droving and did a butchering trade and he was a fairly handy vet for those days. He could sew-up cut humans and set bones and was a good judge of a horse and cattle. He was also a bullocky driver but he was no farmer like his family.

When he was still a young man he went to on a station owned by a man named Devlon. His job was doing the killing and looking after a prize bull as droving had stopped. After some time he was managing the place. It was here that he met Gran at Temora, she was seventeen and they were married at Wagga Wagga. They had three children and they lost one named George. Dad was born years later.

There was Nel and Harry who were much older and they lived on that place for years. Gran told me quite a lot of yarns about that place. Some I have forgotten over the years but here is one I remember well.

Harry was the eldest and when he was very young he would watch Grandad groom the big pure bread clydesdale stallion. But one day he sneaked off to the stable and crawled under the door. After some time Gran missed him and went searching for him, she found him under the horse's legs as he had been brushing away the flies. The horse was standing quiet and Harry had fallen asleep but Gran didn't panic.

Very quietly she called him and said *"Come I have a lolly for you"*. Needless to say he came out quick.

The horse only had to lift one leg or place his foot onto Harry and it would have been, *"Good night kid!"*

On this same station Dad was once getting their prize bull ready for the local show at Wagga Wagga. He thought he was a very quiet bull as he was a purebred milking durum. Dairying had just started in the district. Anyway, the bull must have been on the cranky side and he got Dad up into a corner and gored him in the groin. Dad managed to crawl under the stable door and he was in hospital for some time. After that he always had a slight limp and never did much more hard riding.

THE DOG FIGHT

I heard a fiddle wailing helped along with a hobnail boot,
while somebody played the mouth organ accompanied by the flute.
'Tis the kind of music you hear that makes a country dance,
all 'round the corn barn gathered to the old tunes they loved to prance.

This barn stood in the clearing surrounded by the scrub,
but it only took a horse ten minutes to reach the nearest pub.
Just after dark it started, everyone had bought their dog,
while some sat on the barrel, others set fire to the log.

Everything went steady 'till the first waltz was half way through,
then the kids started a dogfight, you never heard such a hullaballoo.
They dogs that were getting' a hiding, so's to get away from harm,
laid their ears back 'round their collars and headed for the barn.

The floor was mighty greasy as candle grease can do,
like a pack of scalded tomcats they all came charging through.
The rafters really rattled, as big sterns hit the floor,
I've never seen such a mix-up in a country-dance before.

The boots flew in all directions and the dogs really played that night,
while the kids went racing through the scrub like emu's in full fright.
They gathered after, around the barrel and the dogs they soon forgot,
while some nursed a twisted ankle and some a blistered bot.

The teacher had it easy, no kids to teach next day.
Those old bush mums knew their job and how the kids did pay.
For a big quince stick across our stern,
was then the order of the day.

You stood up for your breakfast and stood up for your tea,
an' you asked the Lords forgiveness down on a bended knee.
So that's my old bush story and believe me most is true,
for I was of the jokers that played the big night through.

PUB LIFE ON THE GOLDFIELDS

After some years of hard saving Gran and Grandad bought a pub at Lambing Flat, Gran's brother came with them as a groom and rouseabout. The previous owner was a big Irish man and one of the dirtiest men ever seen. He was a professional rouge and also a drunk and the pub had gone broke. He had lost nearly all his customers and the first thing Gran and Grandad did was to clean the place up and get new beds for the old ones were riddled with bugs.

They had to build a bush house for those getting of the *big binge* (pay day drinking spree). They also had to clean out the rum casks, which had cakes of tobacco in them. After drinking from these the customers were lucky if they knew their own names.

Well after a few weeks it got around that the place was under new management. The shearers and drovers came in the dozen and Grandad really gave them a fair go. Good meals and clean beds along with pure grog. They employed a good Chinese cook and two housemaids and so they had all the custom for miles around.

The customers would hand over their cheques and tell Gran to let them know when they were out of credit. Alec, Gran's brother, would shoot some kangaroos and Gran and Sammy the cook, would make kangaroo soup and put it on the bush house table. The customers would all line up for it and this would go on for some days just giving them a few beers a day and no rum. When they had gone through their credit Grandad would give them a bottle of rum and send them on their way.

The customer's sheep dogs had kennels and were well looked after and this made the old blokes happy. There was a paddock behind the pub where they kept a few sheep and Gran had seen as much as fifty-pound bets on who had the best sheep dog. The paddock and sheep were used to work those dogs and she said that she had never seen a better dog in any Sydney Show that could hold a candle to some of those dogs.

They would also hold buckjump competitions for when the mail coach arrived. These competitions would provide refreshments and meals for those that came in for the mail. The gold miners would pay for their drink and meals with gold dust and nuggets. So Grandad had to be a judge of quality of the gold, which was used to trade. He also had to wait for the gold dealer to buy the gold dust from him before he knew if his judgement had been sound.

At first Grandad got caught out, but it did not take him long to learn, especially with Sammy the Chinese cook to teach him about the gold. It was no time before crooks got short shift and the news soon spread that only nuggets were accepted and not gold dust.

After a few years they sold the pub for a good price and went back to Mamey Johnsons Creek, to his old people and he worked around the stations and farms there. His brother and him then went to Wallamba looking for land with some cedar. They found what they wanted at Dyers Crossing; it was forestland with good brush and the cedar they were looking for.

THE BUSH DUNNY

That word dunny, it puts them city folk to shame.
So they call it a toilet, well that's just another name.
They talk about their toilets, some big an' some are small.
But they don't have our tea-tree bark hooked on a nail up on the wall.

Then I gets a letter from the city the other day.
Me Auntie's coming up the bush for her holiday.

Nulla Nulla

Cecil R. Mackaway

Our dunny of the past, it was just two notches on a log.
But me Aunty from the city was scared of snake and even frog.

So I built a dunny, now I'm one of the very best.
I mostly build 'em low and build 'em facing out nor'west.
Or I can build 'em round with gravel on the floor,
or I can build 'em square with a chaff bag for the door.

Now that dunny that I built would put the city folk to shame.
It didn't have a door nor did it have a chain.
While you sat contented, while the westerly winds did blow,
if you made some funny noises there was no one 'round to know.

Now boxes in the bush are as scarce as hot cross buns,
so I used a smart fork stick on which to rest our bums.
While the roof and walls were stringy bark the can was a big red drum,
and the kids being all excited they tried it, one by one.

To keep the doings nice and to keep the doings clean,
we used a measured cup of good old kerosene.
Well my Aunty came that night all full of friendly air,
and for a good nights sleep she smartly did prepare.

First she must visit the toilet, then she must have a light.
So with a candle in a bottle she strode off into the night.
While she sat there thinking of our hardships away out there,
there came that awful croaking sound out on the midnight air.

This frog, he was a daddy, dark green with big web feet,
as he stood outside that toilet and croaked the Bonaparte's Retreat.
Well the hair stood out upon her neck as she reared up to her feet,
but it was that awful forked stick that stuck firmly to her seat.

Me Aunty was no chicken and this frog was having fun.
She flattened out my dunny and threw the candle down the drum.
You should have seen that fire as it shone out in the dark.
Up went that kerosene then up went that stringy bark.

As for that forked stick, it got stuck between two stumps.
An' it left itself black bruises right across her rump.
Next morning bright and early as she stepped up on the train.
She said, "You can have your frogs and toilet. I won't be back again."

LIVING IN THE BUSH AT KRAMBACH

In some ruins that had belonged to some horse traders there was a big old stone fireplace. The horse traders had stayed there for a while until one was killed falling off a horse, after that they had moved on to Tinonee, which was the only other town about. The three hundred acres at Dyers Crossing were then handed back to the Crown.

Tinonee in the early days at Dyers Crossing had a police station, government wharf, a store and a post office. This was where they arranged to buy the land. There were no roads, only bush tracks for the coaches from Gloucester to Taree and a house or two at Krambach, this is almost the same road that is there today.

There was one *golleg* (public entertainer), her living at Krambach and one little shop, which was owned by an Irish couple. So after the land deeds and business was fixed up my Grandparents rode back to Mamey Johnsons Creek and had a heavy spring cart made. They put one horse in the shafts and one in the outside with an outrigger. They also had two saddle horses and some small items such as a *fountain* (water container), camp oven and a few other bits and pieces.

Grandad drove the horses with some fowl in a coup, slung from under the axel. Alec rode and drove four bullocks and two milking cows. After many hard days travel they made Krambach. It took two weeks to cut a track through the scrub to get to Dyers Crossing and to make it worse it rained for three weeks an there was a flood. No one could get back to Tinonee or Krambach for fresh supplies.

After some weeks camped under a tarpaulin they managed to get to Taree where they were able to get six months of supplies. They had a fireplace and the men felled mahogany trees and cut slabs of shingles. Gran said she cried for two days and it took them six weeks but they built a small dry and warm home.

By this time Granddads friends George Harris and family, with their bullocks and horse, had arrived. Then the next to arrive was the Coils and Tatersal's with a full team of bullocks. They all worked on one place a week at a time until each home was finished and there was enough land cleared for corn and vegies. They grew their own tobacco and used a lot of wild honey.

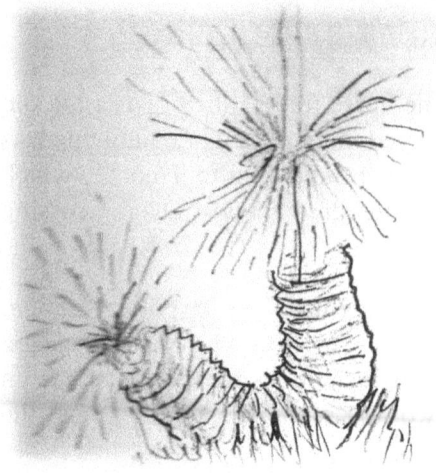

Charley Tatersal had a big bullock dray and they pit sawed cedar and hauled it to Taree where they shipped it to Sydney. In return they would get six months supply of tucker, powders, shot, some rough furniture and some dress materials along with boots, shoes and men's clothes. Alec also shipped koala and opossum skins and this all helped them to get going until they had enough land cleared to start farming.

They farmed mostly corn, which was also shipped to Sydney. By this stage a big shipping company had been built up at the port at Tuncurry where there were warehouses and the place truly bloomed.

The family, Rights, arrived from Sydney. They were *well-up* in the steam engines and boilers and they started a big sawmill and went on to building steam driven boats. They built their own coastal ships and stared a weekly run to Sydney and the place fairly went ahead.

The different families began to arrive; the Startins, Croakers, Gallaghers, Hoys, Averys, Sniders, Maurers, Dyers, Patersons and Murry's just to mention a few. They all settled on Wallamba, Bunyah and Krambach.

The Breckridges arrived at Failford, which they named and they started a big mill store, blacksmith shop, coach building and boat building. Most of these people were either Irish, Scottish, German or English but there were a few *Yanks*. The Brecks also built flat-bottomed boats with steam engines, to come up to a wharf and store house. This is now known as the bullock wharf.

Businesses and home farms started at Nabiac and one of the big drawcards was the pub and boarding house. By now the roads were beginning to take shape and by this time Grandad and Gran were quite settled.

George Harris owned the next block and he grew corn on Grandad's place for a while. About then dairying started and a butter factory was built at Tinonee. Then the Harris's, Jim and George, stared a wagonette business.

They carted cream and delivered goods to and from the bullocky wharf to the stores. They had four big wagons and sixteen horses.

It was about this time that Dads brother Harry got himself married and took over the farm. Grandad did a bit of cattle dealing, veterinary work and learnt the trade of boot-making from Ernie Gorten who lived at Nabiac. Ernie made boots and shoes and did all the *saddlery* and harness work.

Aunt Nel married a sleeper cutter from New Zealand who later joined the police force and was shifted to the Tweed River where they reared a family of five. My dad was born later in life.

When he was old enough he was put to an apprentice engineer at the Dyers Crossing butter factory which had just started and where he worked for about forty years.

Dairying was in a big way in the district and the Tatersal's started a butchery. Grandad spent twelve months with them until they learnt the trade as he was a first class butcher.

The post office was also built at Dyers Crossing and Gran had a lot of midwife experience on the stations. She bought over one hundred babies into the world from Krambach to Bulahdelah. She would walk for miles through the bush, though sometimes in daylight she would ride side-saddle.

Grandad died at the age of 56yrs and his old dog fretted and died three weeks later. He would not even eat for Gran and he howled every night. He was a faithful old *bluey* (cattle dog).

We buried Grandad at Krambach and there was a terrible trouble with the will. The place was sold to the Eastons and then the Patersons, where a young Paterson had half share and Astel Avery had the other. Gran was left with only one acre of land and the old house. It was a very nasty story and I will not go into it here.

Gran was a marvellous woman; she battled on alone when dad was still a boy. She got him his apprenticeship and she also took a *dark boy* in under her wing who had arrived into the district. Neighbours had been sent the lad but had not expected him to be coloured and they were going to send him back to the State School but Gran took him in and arranged a apprenticeship for him as a carpenter.

He became a first class builder and built many of the homes on the Wallamba, including a new home for Gran and one for Dad when he got married. Yes, Gran took in washing, sold eggs, did house cleaning and shop work for an Indian storekeeper at Koribar, between Dyers and Nabiac.

I was born in the same bed and in the same room as my father and my Gran was the midwife. I weighed three pounds and in those days there was no special gear like humidity cribs. Gran did not think that I had a chance but after fixing mum up she grabbed me and rubbed me all over with warm olive oil and fed me on mums milk and three drops of brandy every hour.

I was kept in a kerosene tin, in the warm air going up from the old open fireplace. Gran cared for me day and night for two weeks with only Dad or Roger the *coloured* lad, to give her a break. Then only for a little while would she leave me as she would not trust them or anyone for very long. Anyway, I learnt to walk and talk before any of the other family of eleven.

When I was two, my parents took me to their new house to be reared with my baby brother, Cyril. But at midnight Dad bought me back as I howled and howled all night for mum. Yes, Gran was my mum as far as I was concerned and she reared me.

Gran told me many of these following stories when I was young and she was still a bright and healthy woman. So you can take it from me that they are true, as she never told a lie as I ever found out.

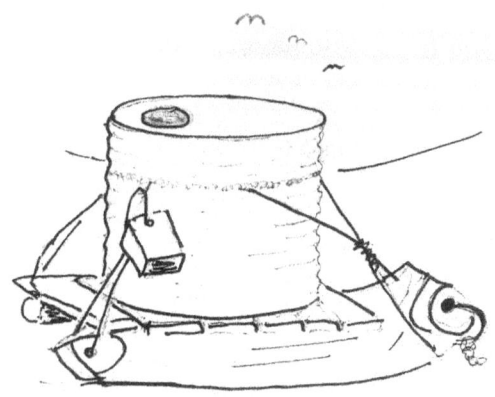

GRAN'S OLD HOME

By a little red house settled a'side a reedy swamp,
I spent many a long childhood day.
Beneath the shade of a big lemon tree I sat,
content I was to watch the baby ducks at play.

With their little heads down,
an' tails turned up, they made a pretty sight.
I spent many happy hours,
until it was getting night.

Then I would gently round them up,
make'em safe from fox and prey.
And from the native cat, the killer,
seldom seen today.

My brothers and I spent happy hours,
beside that shady brook.
With a piece of cotton for a line,
an' bent pin for a hook.

At fourteen I had to go to work,
and become a little man.
But my most treasured memory,
my second mother, who was my dear old Gran.

GROWING UP WITH GRAN

One night when I was seven and it being the middle of the night, our piano began to play. The place was locked up at the time and Gran grabbed a little handbag pistol which her son Harry had given her some years back for protection in the bush. With this in her right hand and the candlestick in the other she slowly approached the lounge-room, afraid of what she might find.

There was this ghost playing, up and down the keys were going all on their own. It was a four-legged ghost though, one who was looking for a mouse. Dad had been down earlier and had played a tune or two on the piano and puss had got onside the piano, likely chasing mice. The cat had been accidentally locked into the piano when Dad had closed it up and left, but it gave us one heck of a fright.

Another time, Gran had attended a birth of one of the Crocker's. She had to walk three miles along a lonely bush track and cross a river twice in the pitch black of night. Some young chaps thought that they would have a joke and so they put a sheet on the end of a pole and as she approached they sneaked it slowly, higher and higher over their heads.

Gran didn't believe in ghosts and called out to who ever it was that they had best to speak up or get going, but up went the sheet a bit higher. So Gran took the little pistol out, aimed above his head or where his head should have been and let go with a shot or two.

Next the pair of hobnailed boots went haring through the scrub taking everything with them and Gran got herself a cheap sheet. She had to mend a bullet hole in it though and needless to say she never seen any more ghosts around Dyers.

Gran loved her garden she always had plenty of vegies and flowers and I remember the old grape vine real well. It was a very old vine and never got pruned, it was only given a bag of cow manure sometimes and it grew all over the quince trees. It was my job to do a spot of climbing and pass the grapes down until Gran had a big enamel colander full and she would wait till the kids were coming home from school and then would take them out and give them a treat.

It was the same with the oranges, plums and passion fruit and she would say that she never had anything stolen. As the kids from school grew up she was looked upon as a lovely old lady and was well respected by them all.

There was a neighbour who selected a hundred acres, he came from the city and had two teams of big draft horses and two big drays. He got most of the road contracts, doing the gravelling and he was a professional thief. He never bought any corn for his horses or vegies for his family.

Grandad had a nice barn of corn but there was one loose slab in the wall and after some time there was one hell of a big hole in the corn. It was Gran who drew Grandads attention to it. As she never took the feed from there and they both had an idea who it may be, so they set a big double spring-ding trap.

That night, just after they put out the house light, they heard somebody really screaming out at the barn. Grandad said to Gran, *"I will leave him there for a while,"* but she made him go and release him. Gran bathed his hand and Grandad put two stitches into it, they never lost any more corn or vegies and once the neighbours knew who it was they would warn him never to go anywhere near their own barns.

It was not long before this that Gran was loosing quite a few fowl but there were no foxes and as the wild cats only sucked the blood, they don't take the fowl, we weren't sure what was going on.

One night we set a trap and it was later that night that a fowl gave a squawk from up in the turpentine tree where they camped. It had a ladder up into it and the tree is still there today (1989). Well Grandad grabbed the old muzzleloader and made for that tree. He arrived to hear boots going through the scrub and there was a bag with six stunned chooks and a pole with a smouldering sulphur rag on one end. This codger would shove the sulphur up under them chooks and down they would come. Well then we caught him in the trap, Grandad made him tell the truth before releasing him... Gran got thirty shilling for her fowls.

I can remember the big shed with the full-length fireplace and the old shingle roof that was still waterproof then. Gran had her sewing machine in there where it was lovely and cool in the summer.

The shed had been made for smoking bacon and as a washhouse, where Gran could boil up a ten-gallon iron boiler with the clothes and the old washing tubs were all up along a rough bench. There was a honeysuckle growing all over the roof and there was also a big wooden trough made from a hollow log, which was used for corning down beef.

Gran would sit over there with her memories and the old side-saddle that had carried her many miles. Just inside the garden gate was three lemon trees, five peach trees, three plum trees, a fig and the old grape vine with the quince trees. I remember a bed spread that Gran crocheted with a fine ninety cotton. It covered a double bed and took her five years to complete.

She did nearly all of it by candlelight and in the centre there was a kangaroo and an emu. It would be worth a fortune today but she sold it to the bank manager's wife for five pounds. The bank manager got shifted to elsewhere a couple of weeks after that.

THE FORGOTTEN FARM

I stand before the big rough gate at the entrance of the yard,
my memory goes back to the cows we milked in the days when we worked hard.
There stands the rusty separator still screwed to an oily block,
an a little shelf that got many a-glance, where was set the old alarm clock.

There was a big school bus to catch and the cream truck on it's way,
and twenty more cows to milk before I could start my day.
There stands the old tallow-wood blocks I used, now covered with dust an' web.
The iron sheet now waves in the wind, that was the roof of the old cream shed.

Down the track towards the house stands the shed an' the old wood barn,
many a night when the stars were bright we husked corn and spun many a yarn.
The harness still hangs on a peg that belonged to Punch and Doll,
you'll find their bones among the grass on the ridge above the knoll.

The rusty plough beside the fence I followed for many a mile,
when I think of the good things we ate it brings back a little smile.
Big melons, they grew on the flat, along with vegies by score.
Back in the big depression, who could ask for anymore.

The old house looked so haunted, lonely, and the roof is falling in,
some was covered in shingles and the other half with tin.
As I stood out there a-dreaming I hear the children by the dam,
and mother by the open fire with a frying pan in her hand.

The rambling rose still blooms and grows outside the smoke house door,
the hooks that held the bacon still lay there upon the floor.
With a sad'ning heart I turn away, from the days we were happy but poor,
but in this big world where so much changes, they may come again once more.

HORSES AND HELP

When I was a baby in arms, me Dad had a trotter, they called him Tommy. Tommy won the trots in most of the country shows and at this time Dad was a little later than usual as he had need to work and as Gran was a great horse woman she decided to take Tommy to Nabiac and enter him in for the trot. She was determined that if Dad could not make it to Nabiac to drive Tommy in the trot then she would race him herself. Dad made it that day but we nearly didn't.

There was Gran, Mum and I in arms and aboard the sulky with Tommy was pulling when we got as far as Nabiac Crossing. Tommy here decided that he wanted to have a drink and that morning he had been fed-to-the-eyes with chaff and corn, and was as fit *'as a fox terrier up a rabbit burrow.'*

While he has a snout under the water and was drinking blissfully when a big mullet flew up his snout and nearly to his ears. Well Tommy gave one hell of a snort, reared and wheeled.

There was this girder beside them, which was part of the footbridge, which crossed the river then. The wheel to the sulky jarred with Tummy's struggles and went up and over the girder, and over went the sulky.

We all landed in the creek and mum was really petrified, she could not get her bum out of the water. Gran still had a grip on the reins and almost had him under control when she glanced around and there was this ugly looking fish in a shawl, which was floating down the river face down. Gran let go to save the shawl and this fish floating face down and Tommy; well he laid his ears back, gives another almighty snort and headed for home with bits of the sulky flying off in all directions.

Some horsemen, also going to the trots, were fortunately able to stop him and bring him back while others living by the crossing took us all in and cleaned us up like new. They recon that I spat up around two gallons of water and half a bucket of sea weed but was soon able to sit up for a drink. I guess I was one tough kid.

The old man won the race that day *by half a mile* but afterwards Tommy went lame. On inspection they drew out a girder slinter which was about four inches long and he went on to get fit and well and won many more races.

Poor old Tommy got bogged in the creek when he was eighteen years old and he *kicked the bucket*. I guess he never really had much luck with that creek but he never again won a race with such a handsome margin.

Talking about horses and droughts, we were all big lumps of kids when we were young and there was one time that Dad bought a lovely grey drought mare. She had a lovely foal who was only four days old but the mare was a bit weak as there was a drought on at the time. This mare went out up to her belly that night, chasing water lilies and she got herself bogged. She was there most of the night.

Next morning we saw the foal galloping up and down the bank whinnying for her. We managed to get her out and set her in a sling but pneumonia set in ah there was nothing we could do, she died quickly.

After this we had the job of teaching this little monster of a foal how to drink his victuals out of the bucket. He was as strong as a horse is supposed to be, only being a daft horse it gave him more horse power under his tail. Well after the four of us, along with some help from mum, and also with spilling twenty or so gallons of milk, we managed to get his head down and into the bucket. It was just as well that he had a thirst up.

As soon as he tasted the milk he gave up the battle and gulped it down like a duck shovelling corn. All the time his tail was swinging around and around like an oversized windmill.

Well from then on he thought he was a dog and not a horse, this as far as he was concerned. We all were his mother and he would follow us everywhere that he spotted anyone of us going.

My sister Joyce, was about eighteen months old when she put her arm around his neck and led him to the fence, then scrambled atop him. He didn't do a thing, just stood there and mum nearly fainted. Arthur, seeing what had happened grabbed a bucket and walked ahead with Bill, the foal following, while Joyce sat atop him like a little monkey without a bridle, saddle or anything.

From then on Joyce rode him everywhere, all over the paddock and around. She would steer him by pushing him on the side of the neck with one hand and then the other. So far all had gone so good and now he came first where us kids were concerned.

Bill always got fed before the *poddies* (baby cows) and he drank early pure milk and ate cracked corn. He would walk up the two steps onto the verandah and get his head into the slop bucket where he would eat all the slops, stale bread, vegetable peels and tea leaves along with any other scraps which mum was trying to save for the pigs.

There was this one-day when mum was feeding the *poddies* and had mistakenly left the dairy door open. On the bench stood a big steel two-gallon bucket full of nice fresh cream, which Bill reckoned that he was more entitled to than the butter factory.

In went the head, but the handle to the bucket was a bit stiff and instead of it laying to one side, this handle stood up. It wasn't until one of us came into the room that he threw up his head and the handle caught over his ears. His head was now stuck fast in the bucket and Bill couldn't see. He panicked! And really wrecked the place with his fear, cans and buckets went flying all over the place and the noise of this frightened him still more.

Swinging madly he hit the separator handle and bent it, then at last he got out of the door and into the open. He ran backwards, around in circles and too-and-throw until he collided with the clothes line post which only jammed the bucket further up his head.

This must have gone on for twenty minutes; it was at least that long until we managed to get the plough rein around his neck and tie it to a post, then pull him short. I climbed onto the fence and managed to get the handle back over his ears but his face was jammed into the bucket and I could see it was bleeding.

Cyril bought me the hammer and carefully I gave the rim of the bucket a real belt and it came off.

Bill never forgot this experience and from then on he ate only grass. He never again looked at a bucket and he never got over his fear of them. He lived to be about nineteen years and became a lovely farm horse, one who was never mouthed but always responded well to the reins.

Grandad didn't dance, as I have said he had a hoppy leg, but Gran was a wonderful dancer. Dancing was the most popular enjoyment in those days. Gran taught many young boys to dance in our district and I would sit for hours when I was a child and play her old cylinder gramophone, one with a big horn. She had dozens of old dance tunes and some are still around in a modern style today.

Gran had a half bulldog bitch, which had puppies near every year. She was a wonderful old pal to me, this dog. It was my job to get the morning sticks and to bring home every evening about thirty ducks out of the big swamp behind the house. Tango, the bitch, always gave me a hand. These ducks were shut up for the night and I would love to watch the baby ducklings standing on their little heads in the duck hole while they chased the water spiders.

One year we lost about fourteen of the ducklings as the duck took them among the clover to catch the bees, but they were stung in the throat and they choked.

As I grew older I spent a lot of time with one of the neighbours, I was like a son to him really. He would break in the bullocks and was also the local vet and he made me a little whip and taught me the old *bullocky lingo...* with many dots and dashes. Gran wasn't at all happy with this and when I saw her go for the big quince stick she always had behind the kitchen door I would really move. Sometimes I would miss out, but others I would wear a mark or two for a few days.

I had very little schooling as I was a very sickly child. No matter what it was, german measles, mumps, whooping cough or scarlet fever, you name it, I caught it. Gran nursed me through the lot with her old bush remedies. At thirteen I went out to work on the local farms, sometimes from five in the morning until eight at night, husking corn.

When my father retired from the factory, the old home was sold and Gran died down there at ninety three. Gran only saw her childhood family once after she was married at Wagga Wagga but most of them were long lived we were told. Some of the family may have more history, if so I will leave the rest to them.

My Gran also had a very sad side to her life as she always spoke her mind but gave help were and whenever she could. No one ever left her place hungry.

There is something I forgot to say – when they were cleaning under the bar of the pub, which they bought earlier on, they found among some old papers sixty pound in a role. It was nearly as much as they had paid for the pub.

TIMBER OF THE PAST

My fondest memories of the bush are a long-way in the past,
Felling bush for settler's way back then, to have themselves some grass.
Now they are growing trees I fear are meant to take the giants place,
but when I remember the waste there was, it puts a frown upon my face.

Sleepers then were cut in thousands, to build them railway tracks,
by many strong hands that held the saw, the wedge, and too the axe.
When the bush we felled was a-burning off back in that fateful day,
many big giants would breathe there last, no longer to moan or sway.

The kookaburra laughed his last good night, from high in their bushy top.
The evening breeze passed them by, when you would see them gently rock.
Them old English castles now, and houses about which our tourists boast,
their timbers were truly our cedar that once grew upon our coast.

No more will you hear the bullockies whip, nor the tickle of the bell.
Nor see those old giant cedars that our Bushmen knew so well.

OLE WORLD DISCIPLINE

You hear people talk about some of the big fish that they catch today; well this is a true story about my brother and myself.

The Wallamba River is fresh water to Dyers and beyond, and it has some of the biggest black eels you will find in any place in Australia, good perch also.

When I was a schoolboy we, my brother and I, would go to the butter factory where Dad was the engineer there and he would give us a penny. Then we would go to the store and buy a big hook. The butter boxes were made at the factory and the timber came in bundles, which were tied together with clothesline rope, three foot to each bundle.

I often now think of the waste, all the rope and twenty pound salt bags that were pelted down over the bank. We would collect it and tie about a dozen lengths of this rope together, then tie a piece of copper wire and a hook at one end. At the butcher shop there was always plenty of hearts or liver and all the scraps that if they were not bought in those days they would go into the boiling down pots for the pigs.

Armed with this big line, a salt bag and a big bullock heart we would go fishing. We would pelt this great line out into the river with a hunk of beef on the end and sit down under the ironwood tree and wait. It would not be long before the rope would be sneaking away and we would let it go for about four feet and hit it, then it would be really on for all.

These eels were about four feet long and as round as a seven-pound treacle tin. Well we were only little fellows but between us, after about twenty minutes battle we would manage to land him, get him into a bag and struggle home to Gran. She would give us three pence for which we got a nice bag of lollies and Gran would boil up the eel for the fowls and ducks.

Our next bit of sport was fishing for perch. We would have a spotted gum or bamboo pole for a rod, an old green cord line or beer bottle cork for a float and bait this with a garden worm or a black cricket. It would not be long before the cork would start to bob up and down but you would wait till it went straight down then pull it straight back over your head. You would meet the perch jumping down the bank to meet you. A good perch would go up to two pounds, but most were about a pound or a little under.

Frogs were another good bait, also grasshoppers. They also would bite at *wobblers* or *spinners* and trout flies. One of the nicest fish in the world to eat is the fresh caught perch, but those days are now gone. When the farmers started using sprays and *super*(phosphate) it got to be washed into the river. They also felled the scrub around the banks and so the perch slowly disappeared.

My Gran was a kind old dear, but discipline and truth came first. Every time I played up or told her a lie I would be in real trouble. Unfortunately, us four elder boys had something of the outlaw in us so Gran made sure she always had a big quince stick handy and she would use it too. She has bought the blood onto me but then I really looked for it too as you will see in my next story.

As I mentioned before, her side-saddle was her treasure. Gran and Granddad would ride all the way down to the Mamey Johnsons Creek to the old peoples place and Grandad would carry my Dad in front of him, on a cushion, when he was a child. They also would often ride to Wingham or Taree.

After Grandads death you can only but imagine how much Gran treasured that saddle of Grandad's as it bought back so many happy memories of their life together. Well on this day Gran went to work at the shop, Cyril and I got down this saddle and had it and the bridle on the top of the rail of the fence. The bridle was around the post and we were playing buck

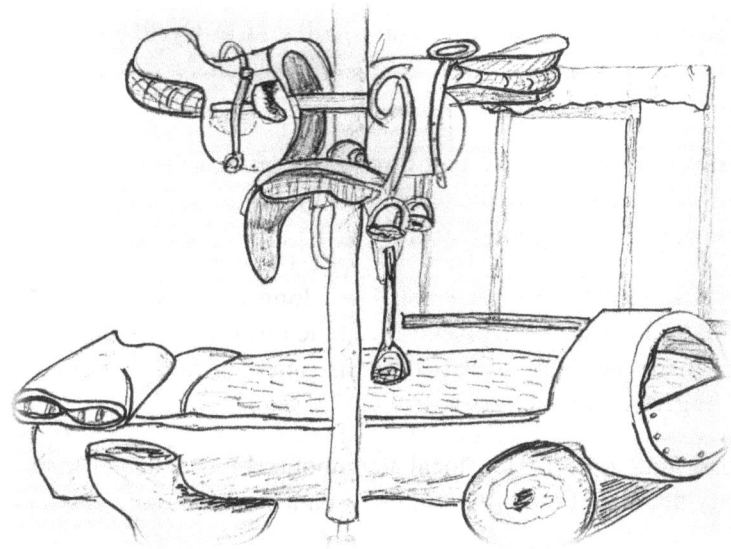

jumper riding. Then I got the big idea that the big horn on the front of the saddle did not look right so I grabbed the hand saw and cut it off.

It was a few days before she noticed it and I came into the room to see her crying. It was the first time I had ever seen Gran cry. After a while she called me to her and asked, *"Who cut the horn of my saddle?"*

As I said before, you could never tell her a lie or you would be sure to get another hiding. She grabbed the stick and took me by the neck, she really went mad and I had marks from my shoulders to my backside and in some places blood. But somehow I managed to get away from her and ran up to my mum.

Gran followed and grabbed Cyril, mum had to pull her off and I stayed there until dad came home and he took me back to Gran's and cooled her down. Dad got that saddle repaired at the saddlers and I was a sore boy for many days. One thing though, we behaved for a long, long time after that.

On another occasion Cyril and I were fishing and when we got back to Grans we still had a cricket on the hook. There was a big old Muscovy drake who stayed just outside and I said to Cyril. *"Watch me catch this big fish."*

So I threw him the line and as ducks like crickets, I got a good bite from the drake. The hook went right through the soft park of his beak and he was really pulling and flapping.

I heard Gran coming down the hall so I said to Cyril, *"Put your hand on him while I get the pliers from the shed."* And there was Cyril, hanging on to this drake and laughing his head off when Gran came onto the scene.

Cyril dropped the rod and shot through as quick as ever when he seen her, while I appeared out of the shed with the pliers to cut the hook from the drakes beak. I was a good boy and Cyril was the outlaw.

Well Cyril kept out of her reach for a long time, but one day about two weeks later he was at the biscuit tin in the kitchen when she sprang on him. He got it for the duck and also for the pinching fancy biscuits, which she saved to give to the visitors with a cup of tea.

Grandad and some of the local neighbours built a dance hall on the old property and they were able to hold a dance each month. It was mostly for the local charity and the Church of England, as well as the Catholic Church at Krambach. There was plenty of music and they would take Gran's good old German piano up on a slide to the hall. They also had about six good violinists and an accordion and concertina player and they all took it in turns to play.

There was also a special room set aside with beds for the babies and a kitchen with all the gear and a big table and open fire place for the card players. People came as far away as Wootton, Failford, Nabiac, Krambach and Bunya, all by sulky or on horseback.

Grandad could not dance but Gran always had plenty of partners. She taught many young ones how to dance then. These dances would start about seven and end at daylight the next morning and there was always plenty of good old country cooking. They had lovely bench stools all around the hall and when I was just a kid Gran had one of these at home.

Dad, Aunty Nel and Uncle Harry sat on it when they were kids. It would have to have been my favourite seat especially in the winter when it would be out on the verandah facing the morning sun. Well after I started school we had a few lessons on chip-carving and one morning I was sitting there on that bench with a chisel in my hand an it was nice and sharp. It was an old winters morning and the sun was lovely and warm, it was such a comfortable spot and I got this gibe idea that I would do myself a bit of chip-carving.

It was really going great but then Gran spotted me, though I did not hear anything until the big quince stick came fair down on the middle of my back.

I landed on the lawn in one jump and never seen that chisel again, not even after I grew up. I have an idea that she may have dropped it into the duck hole and the old stool that stood in the sun from so many years is now with my daughter Bon. It has been on every farm and place of work of mine all my married life and with lick we may see my wife and my golden wedding soon. So the old stool has been around and seated bums of every shape and size over the years.

When I was about twelve years of age Gran bought me a lovely new bike. She gave twelve pounds cash for it, which was a lot of money in those days. One day I was riding up to my mates place in Germany Lane and there was this down hill run to the barn from the house. I got this bright idea that we could find out who could ride the best. So I started going flat-out at the barn and we was going to see who could pull up the closest to the building. We both had back pedal brakes and I sure remember moving real fast.

When I woke up later my mate and his Uncle were pouring water on me and the front wheel and fork of that bike of mine had parted company. What a mess my brand new bike was.

Dad was handling us now and he was worse than Gran was when he got going, which wasn't too often thank goodness. The Uncle had an old bike and he used this to rebuild mine. He plastered some red pain on it so as it would look new and I told Gran that I had lent it to Mr Maurer to ride to work as his horse had galloped over his. I had ridden my mate's bike home and Gran just smiled and said that I was a good boy and that it had been a nice thing to do. Well she never did learn the truth and I rode that bike right up until the time I got married.

OLD FRIENDS

There's a neat little home that's nestled where the head of the Manning flows,
where the night owls call as the shadows fall like they did some years ago.
Sitting there in her easy chair dreaming of the past,
when mustering day was no holiday, you had to be young and fast.

When she and her man would muster cattle up within the hills,
wild riding was everyone's pleasure, never thinking of the rocks and spills.
Yes she was one of my mates from school, of many long years ago,
when we all marched along together, where the old Wallamba flows.

Her father was one of the neighbours from the back in those depression days,
when we lived on parrots and damper an' a breakfast of fine ground maize.
He loved his cattle and horses, he was one of the stars in the show,
he had cups and ribbons in the dozen, but that was a long time ago.

As a young man he helped me, they both did the best they could,
they taught us to stick together and take the bad along with good.
Now my little school friend, we wish you the very best,
may good fortune be with you, and your little house towards the west.

THE FAIRER SEX

Another time when there was seven of us boys and four of the girls, we all would walk about two miles to the school through the paddocks. Just down the hill, below the school, was a big dam and I recall it had been a very hot day.

At lunchtime we made it up that we would wait till the teacher rode off on his old Harley motorbike and that when the girls were over the next hill, we would strip off and have a good old swim in that dam. Some of the girls must have overhead us though as we was making our plans.

When the teacher took off and disappeared around the bend, and when the girls also disappeared, we went for that swim. We were having the time of our lives until someone looked up and then yelled, *"Here comes the teacher!"*

He had a pole about six feet long and was waving it madly about in the air. Well you should have seen the movement; some were in shirts and carrying their trousers, some had one leg in their pants and carrying their shirts and all the tucker-bags were still on the bank. There was a lot of the kids with belly-aches from the punishment of missing dinner the next morning but we still had to face the music at school the next day.

To make matters worse, the girls had been hiding behind a big tree and they were laughing their silly heads off. We had to stay in at lunchtime and do a hundred sums. I they were not right or not finished then we had to stay each day until we had them right and finished in time. Believe me, there were some hungry kids at dinnertime.

My biggest embarrassment though was when I was just sixteen and I was working for a farmer, getting one pound a week and my keep. This was good money and by now I was a fair farmer myself. I had started working at thirteen and I had to grow all the crops such as corn, sorghum, oats, potatoes, pumpkin and grammas and some of the vegies also.

The lady of the house grew the dainty stuff and the two of us were milking forty cows by hand. This meant a 4:30am start of a morning and I had managed to save ten pound, besides buying myself some really *lairy* clothes.

I had also bought my first motorbike, a two speed Douglas, second hand, with a belt drive and no clutch. After you pushed it for about a hundred years, flat-out it would fire with a bang, which sounded like a twenty-five pounder gun. Then it would take off, this was when you had to be more active as you had to jump for the saddle. Sometimes you would miss and land on the rack behind and sometimes it really bolted and you could only but try to hold it while you were taking strides about ten feet long until at last you and the bike would hit the road together.

A pretty little girl in Nabiac took a fancy to me, this young lair; so all dressed up in a double breasted coat with twenty-four inch bottomed oxford bag trousers and an expensive Stetson hat, I braved up enough courage to approach her parents for permission to take her for a ride on my shiny new machine.

After about ten minutes spent giving me instructions on my behaviour we were allowed to go a short way only, this about four miles. To be a true gent I could not expect this lovely darling to make a mighty spring onto the big iron rack where she was to sit. So we had to find a suitable hill to run down, an' yes... there was one about half a mile away.

It was a dirt road and it had rained the night before. By the time we had pushed this monster to the top, in the mud, we looked great! The bottom of my twenty-four inch bags had enough mud on them to fill a grave and my dancing pumps, which had been really glittering, were now in a real mess. My shirt was all sweaty and my tie was nearly around the back of my neck.

When we got to the top of the hill we just stood and looked at one another, she looked nearly as bad as me and then she started to laugh at me, and this monster machine.

"Next time..." she told me, *"Ride your push bike!"*

Yet, undeterred, we mounted for the fray and I put the monster into neutral and let her go. When I jumped her into top gear she let out one might bang and I thought for a moment that she had blown off her muffler. The girl, my darling, nearly fell of with fright but things settled down lovely. My girl had both arms around me like an octopus and after about two mile we came to some bush and had just started up a little hill when the belt on the monster broke.

Well my girl panicked when we stopped, as she reckoned that I had did it on purpose. I was trying to explain when along came their neighbour in his truck, he had just delivered a load of pigs to Wingham bacon factory and she waived him down and then climbed aboard and took off. She never spoke to me again.

I had to push that monster home and was late for work. I ended up having to pay the *Missus* ten shillings to have my clothes cleaned up and after that I left farming. I went out with the men, sleeper and brush cutting and I never farmed again until after I got married.

Yes, in those days you were not considered a man until you could smoke, and you were not ready to take the girls out until you had some down on your chest. Cyril and I had neither, so I decided to learn to smoke first. After some instruction from an old German friend who grew his own tobacco, on how to make a good *corn-cob pipe* we went to work.

We made a couple of *beaut's* and now we were ready. The old bloke gave a grin and said; *"Now I had better show you how to load them."*

But first a bit about this tobacco, this *bloke* would pick about a dozen big leaves and then he would make a big hamburger out of them. He would spread a mixture on each leaf, one of brown sugar, rum and saltpetre. Then he would stick them together and press them in a wood vice for over a week. Each day screwing up the vice a bit until in the end he would have one big cake of tobacco which would knock a bull of its feet.

Well, we were all blowing smoke around like the *north coast mail train* while the *old bloke* was sitting back in his armchair with a grin not unlike the *cat that ate the canary*. It wasn't long before the world started to spin and when we looked at one another we were going a slight *shade of green*. We threw the pipes over the verandah and headed for our bikes but we never made it. We hit the ground and bought up some of the Christmas dinner we'd eaten two years before.

The *old bloke* had a good laugh and after a while gave us a cup of water and told us to throw the pipes in the river. We never started smoking again until I was around thirteen and then only on light Capstan cigarettes.

When I was a young fellow, my father in-law that was-to-be had a big black draft horse. This horse was really in a big trouble as he could not make water because he had a big wart on the end of his *pissel*. After much thought the old man got a big paint brush, dipped it into spirits-of-salts and after speaking very softly, an in a shaky voice, he approached the trouble spot with much caution and quickly dabbed the spirit-of-salts onto the trouble spot.

Now he had a plough rein around the monsters neck, which he hung onto with his left hand while he performed the delicate operation with his right hand. Things went quiet for a few seconds, and then things really happened. There was one great snort and a funny gurgling sound from the horse's back passage. He dug his back hooves into the ground and then he took off!

The *old bloke* hung on like a leech to a bawdy steer but after being *sniggered* for a hundred yards Pop decided that Neddy was a bit stronger than he so he let him go. The paddock had about one hundred acres and Neddy bucked, snorted and backfired from one end to the other. After some time he got his second wind, he arced his back like a camel then started to piddle. It was near a vegie garden an' he washed out about a dozen tomatoes.

I am pleased to say that he was completely cured but don't say *'paint brush'* anywhere within his hearing or he will bolt regardless of anything that could be behind him.

THE GHOST OF GOANNA GULLY

On the way from Dyers to Krambach there was a little gully with a footbridge and they called it Goanna Gully. We had an old neighbour that was one of the best at telling ghost stories and we loved to listen to him.

They had an old home with a big open fireplace and on a winter night us boys would go over and sit while the old chap would tell us bushranger and ghost stories. By the time we would have to go home our teeth would be rattling but it didn't stop us from going.

The best story was about the Goanna Gully ghost. Many years back there were timber cutters camped there and both of them disappeared. The only clue was bloodstains outside of their hut and on some night there were these awful groans to be heard near the creek. As time went on and we grew older the ghost of Goanna Gully was forgotten and we rode our bikes past the place on many nights, it became quite a normal event.

This night there was a circus in Krambach and we all went along for the entertainment. On our way home the weather came up, it was pitch dark with a heavy wind and when we arrived at the gully there was this plank that spanned the creek. We had to get off our bikes and were carrying them

across this plank when all of a sudden there was this most awful groan as I ever heard.

Well if you have ever seen two blokes peddle, it was us! *Hopman* would not have seen our dust. I did not go home to Gran's that night but *dossed* in with my brother and we both covered our heads. We did not say anything to Dad as he would have gone crook and have told us not to be stupid but we told Mum.

She always liked a joke, an' she really laughed and said that the bones of the cutters were there somewhere. Gran backed up what she said by saying that the famous *Fishers Ghost* had vanished after they had found his bones. Even the neighbour said that the ghost had chased him on a white horse, groaning all of the while.

After about a week, on a nice sunny day, which was with a sea breeze we decided to go look for this ghosts old bones. The bones would have been about eighty years old by now so we didn't know what to expect. While we stood on that haunted ground it all seemed to be so close and it wasn't long before we dropped our bikes and bolted through the paddock.

We met an old farmer who was repairing his fence and as we were almost out of breath and scared out of our wits, he was ready to hear what we had to say. We told him the whole story and then about the ghost chasing our neighbour on a white horse. He pretended to look really scared and I'm sure he nearly choked when he turned his back, but he said it was a ticklish throat from smoking too much.

It seems he had heard about our corncob adventure so to oblige us he would go back with us to collect our bikes. Well we did not have to wait long when we got there and the moaning was as loud as ever. We were glad to have a close a friend but the framer laughed and said that these ghost tales were jut people having fun, that there was no such thing.

He pointed up into the big blackbutt trees that spread above our heads and said, *"Now see that big limb growing over the limb of the other tree, well when the wind blows they rub together."* Sure enough, he had hardly stopped talking with it happened again.

We found some old cow bones and took them home and told Mum, Gran and our neighbour that we had found a complete skeleton. That took the grin off their *dials*.

THE GOANNA GULLY GHOST

All kids love the stories that the old folk used to tell,
some, they were so scary they were much too scared to tell.
This ghost he was a special breed that haunted Goanna Gully,
and anybody that went that way was always in a hurry.

He had an awful groan just like a dying cow,
and that awful groan that rasped, I still remember now.
My brother and I on speed wheels rode in a little place called Krambach,
forgetting about that awful ghost that haunted the lonely track.

His head cut off at neck, by some old and murdering brute,
just to get his watch an' chain, and a pair of hobnail boots.
He must have died in torture for his groans were loud and clear,
that's a story we remembered as we approached that place with fear.

'Twas just as we crossed that gully and headed straight for home,
It came, that sound we dreaded, that awful mournful groan.
Me brother he was a rider, fit for any track,
my eyes were nearly blinded from the stones he had kicked back.

Telephone posts were flying past like sleepers on railway tracks,
an' there he was behind us, as I took a quick look back.
At last I saw our welcome home but I'll never will forget the sight,
I'll not forget that daring ride we did on that starry night.

Next day was bright and sunny and we were as brave as Ned,
we'd find that ghost in the gully, for sure with or without a head.
As we stood beside the gully up came a little breeze,
then that awful groan which could be heard, left us shaking at the knees.

O'er our heads were the gum tree limbs, rubbing, one again' the other,
we had found ourselves that awful ghost, me and my little brother.
An old white horse was near the road nibbling at the grass,
he was the white headed ghost that had scared folks of the past.

IN THE GOOD OLE' DAYS

In the good old days, when we were kids, that's the days when they made real movies of people and not space junk, sex and more sex. The days when Cyril and I were young, when Tom Mix and Charley Chaplin were the best shows, and a kiss sounded like a bloke pulling a cork out of a champagne bottle. There was this chap that had an old Ford, fitted up at the back with an old *kero'* engine and a generator that was big enough to supply Taree with power. He used to back this up to the front door of the old Nabiac Hall and believe me; he showed some really good pictures.

He had a good piano to play the sound affects and there was some of the funniest noises. We would have to give this old engine a crank and then it was all on. As I said, it was when a kiss seemed like some bloke had pulled a cork out of a bottle, what a smack!

Then there was those back-fires of the old engine and when the wind blew it into the hall, well it was hard to see if it was Tom Mix or Donald Duck, for all the *kero'* smoke.

When all the excitement was over it was time for the nightmare ride home. Four miles of it, pitch-dark, no light, loose gravel and potholes you could bury a horse in. The old bikes in those days weighed half a tone and often times you would be riding on a flat tyre. They were real bikes!

Down the lane to Gran's was a fairly steep hill, but I knew every blade of grass on it. This night, after being down at the pictures, I was really hiking down there, but an old cow had decided to have a snore right there on the track.

Well she must have heard me coming as she had got to her knees when I hit her amid ship. There was this great blurt from each end and when I picked myself up some twenty feet further down the hill the only damage was one completely ruined front wheel. The poor old moo was sure to have a miscarriage or at least a bellyache, believe me I took more care thereafter.

Just after my wife and I were married, we were still really just big kids, still nineteen and still playing silly games. Gran decided to teach Muriel how to make homemade bread. We were living with Gran at the time.

Potato yeast was the thing at the time and Gran had a very old bottle, which really made it with enough kick to flatten a horse. Of course there was plenty of flour in the concoction and this day, when the mixture was ready, Muriel asked me to remove the cork. To be funny I give the bottle a good shake and asked her to hold the bottle while I cut the string.

In those days she had beautiful black hair that fell to her waist and with a stupid grin I cut the string. There was one almighty pop and there was Muriel, with just two beady eyes glowing fierce through the white flour mask. Her hair was like a polar bears which had been through a snow storm and the ceiling was white for feet around. Believe me, I was not the most popular bloke on the river for over a week.

I was the third bloke to have a wireless around Dyers, it was a two-valve set and we could get 2NC well at night and 2KM on a clear winters night. It had earphones but I later got a little cone speaker and this wireless hung on the wall like a photo frame. It used to have a good audience on Friday night.

The *Wrestle's* (ring wrestling) were on with Big Chief, Skull Murphy and many others. Jack Davey was the great announcer of the day and he used to get all excited and would say there was blood all over the place. He had many saying such as *"Now they are tied up in so many knots that I don't know one for the other. Here is trouble, an old girl has just flattened the skull with the knob of her walking stick!"* or *"He is still out."* And *"The Doctor is still in attendance. Yes it is all over." "The police are still in the ring, they are pouring water by the bucket full on the skull. Yes his coming around. He's been given a decision on a foul. The crowd has gone mad!" "Yes there is a brawl started in the crowd and the police have their hands full tonight!"*

We had old time dances for one hour every Friday night. Then we had Aider and Elsie, Blue Hills and Dad and Dave. Another good announcer was Bob Dyer and his 'Pick a Box'. Bob and Davey were great friends. Bob and his wife were also champion fisher-people and they had a lovely boat.

My aerial was the longest and highest on the Wallamba. I would attach a big knot to the end of a quince stick, then throw it, with a fishing line attached, over a gum tree which was about 200 feet high. I would then attach a wire and pull it over and attach the other end of the wire to a pole at the house, using insulators at every join. The distance was about seventy yard and we got great results.

My first car was an old T-model Ford, which I bought for seven pounds, and with Keith Martins help I made a utility. My brother and I were doing some scrap-iron hauling and we had a big load of old farm gear taken from a creek, which had a very steep bank. The old T-Ford tipped up and there we were, sitting up in the air with the tail of the truck on the ground. The hand break was of no use so as soon as we loaded it in she came down. We then chocked the wheels but she jumped the chocks and nearly ran over the pair of us, then ended up in the creek herself.

I am pleased to say that she was tough and there was no serious damage. So with a lighter load she made the grade and we had the big job of carrying the rest of the load up the bank and then we were able to go on our happy way.

Another time during the big depression I was ploughing a big flat and breaking in western draft horses to work in pairs. I was earning one pound a week and one meal per day. It came to Saturday and I was working half day, I was supposed to collect my one-pound and bring back something to eat from the store. All we had in the house at the time was a little rolled oats, which we had eaten for breakfast and there was no dinner, we were all very hungry. In those days you did not borrow from your neighbour as we were all *in the same boat*.

So when I unharnessed the horses the Boss came down and said that he was sorry, but he did not have the pound until Monday. I had never stole anything in my life but when a man sees his kid's hungry he gets desperate.

I knew there was an acre of swede turnips, which a bloke was growing for his pigs an' I pinched a sugar bag full that day. We had them fried, boiled, baked; you name it we ate it until Monday. Some time later I told the famer what I had done and he said, *"Roy, I hope it filled a hollow spot."*

THE PICKLE BOTTLE POULTICE.

It was back in the Depression when things were pretty crook.
You had no money to pay the doc' so took lessons from a book.
I gets a double-header boil on the near side of me goat,
and the only solution to me trouble was to wear me long an' dusty coat.

Now in our double barrel bed things were getting pretty hot,
me eyeballs seemed to meet every time I tried to cough.
Me Missus, she wasn't fussy 'bout where she put her knees
she had me turning an' twisting like I had the flea's.

Now me Grandpa was a man of very high renown,
he had a head just like a walrus an' loved most women 'round our town.
At last I was full exhausted and feeling mighty crook,
I let this blue-eyed joker, have a good long an' troubled look.

I pulls me pants around me boots, shuts me eyes with certain fear,
I let him poke his long skinny fingers around me tortured rear.
At last with many grunts he went on to explain,
yep you can fix that big red monster, without the slightest pain.

After given me full instructions on how to save me life,
I goes home in awful torture and tells me darling wife.
She listens very careful and gives a funny look,
Yes I have seen such a poultice, in our doctors book.

After some funny noises, and a grin she tried to hide,
down came the pants in a hurry and across the bed I l'yed.
Down the hall an' in the kitchen, behind the kitchen door,
she had bottles by the hundred she'd saved from the year before.

As I heard the bottles rattle, my heart did miss a beat,
as she tried them out, one by one, and then made a quick retreat.
At last she found a pickle bottle, that would do a alright job,
She said, "This will really work, I am game to bet ten bob."

On the fire was a kettle an' the water was boiling hot,
she heated up the pickle monster, then slapped it on the bot.
I've seen birds pull grubs from wattle but as quick one would wink,
half of my bum went down that bottle an I can't say I didn't blink.

I gave one awful scream like a curlew I the night,
That cat, he flew for cover and nearly died of fright.
That bottle hung on like a bulldog as I yelled an' jumped an' screamed,
while me pants that worked like hobbles were stretching at the seams.

My Grandpa, he's dead and gone now,
may the angels bless his soul.
For he's the only man this side of hell,
that's got a Grandson with two bum holes.

THE DREADED PICKLE POULTICE

The pickle poultice is short for pickle poultice murder. Yes, it was not long after we were married that I got this double-header boil on my *goat*. After the wife had made many inspections, one day she says, *"It's ready for a poultice."*

Now some of the old tough folk would often speak of the kind of poultice invented by Louis Stevenson. You pour boiling water into a pickle bottle, then you pour the water out and clamp it on the boil while the steam is still in the bottle. Believe me, these bottles grab and hang on but they do not say that you have to be dead drunk before or the horror of it is all the worse.

Well down comes my pants around me boots and across the bed I lay. Muriel clamped the bottle on and man; with-in two seconds flat half me bum went down that bottle. The agony is something no man can explain and here I am jumping around with this bottle swinging about like a milking machine cup. Me trousers tripped me up and down I went onto the floor and bang went the boil. It was the cleanest job you ever saw but I had a hole in me bum as big as an eggcup. It really worked, but take my advice and have someone knock you out before you try it!

OLD TOM

Old tabby Tomas sat on a fence, for he had little else to do,
his fighting days were over and romance was quite taboo.
He wore battle scars from head to tail, his fur a patchwork rug,
his ears were split, his eyes were red, he had the look of a punch drunk pug.

As he groomed his whisker his memory slipped back to the past,
when he roamed the bush for parrots and caught field mice in the grass.
He has children by the dozen all up and down the creek,
he was loved by all the ladies, he was the Manning River sheik.

Many the grain of buckshot the boss removed from 'round his tail,
the pain from the cuts and bruises really made him wail.
But now he's a retired tomcat, the boss feeds him on the best.
No more he'll hunt for parrots and he gets a good nights rest.

So let us be like old tabby and enjoy life while we can.
And while we have a free Australia, let us trust the younger man.

THE HOT CAT

Tomas was a big black and white tomcat who belonged to our neighbour, and he was the greatest thief known to the cat world. He would visit our place often and Mum gave strict orders never to feed him after he pulled a hot roast off the kitchen table once.

Cyril and I decided it was time that we gave him short shift so we got a piece of rag and dipped it into *kero*, tied this to his tail and struck a match to it. Being after dark it really glowed in the night and the cat, he got moving around in circles for a start and then straight up under the house. Flames were really flying but it was good luck that our house was on high blocks.

Thomas raced around under there for a bit and then headed home. There, their house was really very old and almost on the ground and we could see ourselves by this stage, doing life in gaol. The place would *go-up* for sure but to our greatest relief the rag burned out a few feet from their verandah and we never, after that, had any trouble from Tomas.

MY FRIEND WILLY

Willey is a wagtail and Tomas is our cat,
I often have a laugh at the games that they get at.
Tomas give a yawn as he stretches himself, along out in the sun,
while Willy thinks this is the day to really have some fun.

So he waits 'till poor old Tomas is really fast asleep,
then he lands right beside him and lets out that awful screech.
Thomas opens up one yellow eye and looks him in the face,
awhile his tail is a revving like a swallows wings in space.

Willy gives a flutter and lands himself up along the line,
while Tomas's eyelids drop once more, and his tail stops beating time.
Just as Tomas's gone back to sleep and dreaming of the past,
Willey lands right up beside him and give him another blast.

Tomas gives a hiss, then rears high, up to two feet tall,
If ever I catch that screeching brut I'll eat him, feathers, beak an' all.
He heads off then along to the lounge and finds the softest seat,
and like all good, lazy tomcats he's soon back fast-asleep.

A FLIGHT, WITH BLUE HEALER POWER

My brother was a bit of a Casanova and he was pretty friendly with a girl who was working for a local farmer. They planned together that she would leave her bedroom window open and so about 11pm he faced his big adventure.

The two blue healer dogs did not hear him on the verandah where the window was open, and there she was reading the paper. So not unlike a first class burglar he had one leg over the windowsill with the paper dropped and a big voice yelled at him, asking who the hell he was!

He went through the wrong window that night and things really happened. It was *"go-man-go"*.

He dived off the verandah and headed for the road to his bike but the blue healers had heard the racket and they gave chase. It was just his good luck that he got a flying start but there was a fence with five barbed wires strung along it. He took a header and all that was left of his shirt was the neckband. He had scratches from his head to his bum. His story when he finally got home was that he was pelted into the blackberry bush off his bike.

TALKING CORPSES

A talking corpse makes a horses snort, and there is nothing you can do,
but hang on with hands and heels, an' by the seat o'your britches too.
Riding by a boneyard, and just for a little joke,
he said, "How 're you all sleeping there?" Then the corpse he really spoke.

He answered, "Not too bad."

Now to get an answer from a ghost, or even someone just departed,
that horse, he really bucked and reared, cocked his tail and really farted.
The blade of grass beside the log was almost three foot high,
where the local drunk was sleeping as the lad went riding by.

That nag, he's gone so spooky he has to be blindfolded every night,
in case the echoes of his snorting kills the brute in awful fright.
The ol' boneyard up at Krambach, it's been there for many years,
it has seen many handshakes, greetings, old yarns and many tears.

One old bloke for Dyers Crossing he had no kin or folk,
so with the aid of a shot gun he thought that time it was to croak.
So they took him up to the boneyard, it was Krambach's resting place,
with no mourners or cheerful Parson, to send him off home in space.

His box was made from hardwood, no silver handles on side or top,
and the hole had filled with water and he went down with a mighty plop.
As the folks removed their hats to say a word or two,
two blue healers got in holds, you never seen such an awful blue.

They fought each'er like demons, or like two monkeys up a pole,
they got themselves unbalanced, then went headfirst down that hole.
So they fished them out with shovels and filled the big hole in,
where the old bloke was sleeping soundly, quite from strife or even sin.

But me Missus has gone all spooky, she's making me hair go white,
digging up me convict relations, all day and half the night.
She had me in every boneyard from here to Muswellbrook,
me eyes have gone all glassy and I cackle like a chook.

So good bye to all them boneyards and them blokes that's sleeping well,
they can shove me through the cooker and drop me ashes down the well.

THE BUSH CAMP

When we were young and had a young family I got a fairly big job of brush felling, and brushing light scrub for two neighbours. It was four miles from the store and in these days the bread and meat was left in a box out on the road, which was two miles away.

My wife decided that she also would go bush with me and she did really do things the hard way in those days. The old cream lorry shifted us out to the site where we camped, beside the creek. Our furniture? It was mostly made of deal boxes and other bits and pieces and Muriel's stove was a camp oven, which she became professional at handling. This oven was over an open fire balanced from a pole and held up by two forks, one at each end of the pole.

Her washing machine was a scrubbing board and a one-bit washing tub, down beside a mountain stream. And to get milk she had to push a pram over a mile with the five other children, up along a bush track.

I had to walk a mile, mostly over a mountain to get to work, as that was as close as the truck could get. It was mostly dark when I got home and we had been there for some time when drought set in. The bush fires began and we were surrounded and could not get out, so one night we lit a fire close by to back-burn and protect ourselves from the fires.

The heat and the smoke was a real trial for us, especially the baby but by morning it had really worked. There were logs and trees still burning for weeks after and the water got pretty bad. You had to boil every drop until some weeks later when we had a storm and a few days rain to flush the creeks.

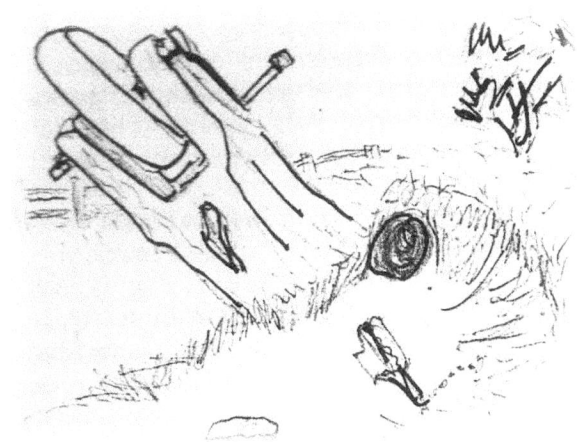

A fairly heavy wind came up with the rain and the night that followed it grew heavier. The ground was still soft and the pegs of our tent all pulled out; so down came the tent onto us all and to make matters worse it was pitch black with no moon. There we were, trying to hold the tent up over the children most of the night and toward the morning I managed to get the centre pole up despite the storm.

Muriel hung on and I don't know how, while I fumbled around looking for the lanterns and a box of matches. At last I found them among the over turned pots and pans and then it was out into the storm to cut long wooden pegs. Near the morning we had everything straightened up again and the storm had cleared up enough for us to get a big fire going and to dry ourselves, and most every other thing. After that I never again trusted pegs that were supplied with a tent. I always cut my own.

Around the campsite there were lovely long blue gum saplings growing all around us. It was wonderful on a moonlit night to watch the big black flying squirrels flying from one to the other tree and the opossums that were all around us. You would hear brush wallabies thumping by at night and sometimes the dingoes would howl quite close by. But we were both good shots with rifles and guns and Muriel really could use the old twelve-gauge gun, as snakes were plentiful.

We got some little white chickens then, and when they started to run around they drew the attention of many critters. This day I heard six shots back at the camp and I got worried so hurried home. Muriel met me with a big grin; she had five *jackasses (kookaburra's)* lined up on a log, all out of the six shots. They had got four of the chickens.

After the rain the big cicadas or black locus started to swarm. They would roar all day and the green ones would take over at nights. These gums around us were their favourite and between the noise and the spray they would send down it was almost enough to send one nuts!

This Sunday, Muriel's sister came out and the racket was so bad that I decided that the closest of the trees had to go. It was a fair sized sapling ad the breeze was blowing in the right direction so it was decided that I should fell it. When I got the belly cut in, something told me to get everyone out of the tent.

We were camped in a valley and it wasn't unknown for the breeze to chop around a bit. True enough, I no sooner started on the back when a heavy gust came the other way and away went the tree… straight into the corner of the tent. It smashed two poles and smashed the tailboard off Muriel's sewing machine, which her parents had given her as a gift. It also broke

some plates and cups and that was the first time I really saw her break down. We both had a little weep for these were the only possessions we had.

After a while we pulled ourselves together and I cut off the tree, cut more poles and the girls sewed up the tent. I gave that tent a coat of paint with oil and later her father, who was a good carpenter, fixed up the machine. Somehow we managed to replace the cups and plates. I studied up on the noisemakers and learnt one thing, a bushman should know never to trust the wind when you are felling a tree.

Living in the bush in those days offered many adventures when the children were growing up. Our lives became enmeshed with the bush and this offered its own sense of home.

At one time the kids developed really big appetites and after some time Muriel got a bit curious about the amount of food they were tucking away. She followed them one day down to the creek, only to find out that they were feeding a big six-foot goanna and she was not pleased. After giving strict instructions that they were not to again touch the big goanna, some of the tucker supply was then, not expectantly, cut off.

After some weeks, *Gwaney*, their goanna disappeared and for a few days the kids were very upset. However next thing the goanna lands right at the tent with about a dozen babies. She must have decided that all would be OK for a feed and these goanna's then ran all over the floor, all over the beds and even up onto the table.

Muriel resorted to the broom to send *Gwaney* and her brood back to the creek and after that the goanna always kept a fair distance from the tent. Eventually, as the babies grew up, they moved back into the bush but for a while we had to live with mum and her brood, ever on the lookout for something to eat.

SNAKEY

Snakes, they are a creepy lot you'll find almost everywhere,
just killing off our bird life and that I do declare.
They eat bird eggs and eat their chicks by hundreds every year.
And bush cats gorge out on birds without the slightest fear.

Now, to all you bird brains out there, what drop cats and harbour snakes.
I hope bugs eat your garden, and from sprays your belly aches.
Then we have them Greenies with a brain, big as a pea.
They wouldn't know an iron bark from a broad leaf stinging tree.

We also have them gum-tree fools that shade their pretty house,
there'll come a Southerly Buster, straight in from down the south.
You'll have gum leaves in your bedroom, splinters on the kitchen floor,
sparks from broken wires will send the joint up with a roar.

So wake up young Australia and use your little brain.
For like some other countries we'll sure go down the drain.

Snakes were also a part of life that you had to learn to cope with. One evening while I was resting and Muriel was washing up, we had an unwelcome visitor to our tent. The lantern was getting short of *kero'* so the light was not too good at the time. Muriel moved to step over a big stick on the floor, which would have been yet another that the kids had bought into the tent, when she thought suddenly that she had seen it move.

Quickly grabbing the brush hook from close-by she pinned it down yelling, *"Snake!"* amid all the commotion. I leapt up from that bed faster than ever and grabbed the torch and spade and beheaded the brute while she pinned him to the floor. You could never be too careful even if it had been a stick.

There was always dozens of fireflies at night also and the children would have the fun of their lives catching these little flying sparks and putting them into a bottle which made a very pretty display.

We would let them play with them for a while and then release them as I explained; they were harmless and would soon die if left in the bottle for long. The kids seem to understand.

The old pram was also a great thing out in the bush, it was a big strong old job with big wheels and it carried the baby, the groceries and the meat and bread which were always left two miles from the road for us to collect. The only other convenience we owned was a pushbike. That old pram also carried the washing to the creek and went over the mountain to get some milk from the farmer. The wheels ended up for a billy-cart for our son to get the morning sticks and wood. It seemed to live on forever.

When I went to work I always took the riffle as there was plenty of wild game in those days. Animals such as pigeons, turkeys and a few rabbits could make a lovely pot of curry or soup. I never let a snake or bush cat go past and I shot everyone that got into my sights.

Some of our lawmakers don't know the first thing about the bush and many mistakes are made. Snakes and cats kill not hundreds of birds each year, but thousands and then we have the pest the fox, which shouldn't be here, and so the result is that the bird life is dying out. The insects are taking over where there weren't so many as before and the sprays that are used are killing the people and the animals. I was instructed by the laws-that-be not to kill the snakes or goannas but there were times when you had to kill.

One day I heard a beast bellowing in pain up a gully, she had got herself bogged while trying to get at water lilies. There were two big goanna's tearing her into pieces while she was still alive and I shot them both and also the beast as she had all her back parts ripped out. When the Boss came riding around I told him what had happened and he was astounded. The same thing could have happened to a man if ever they were knocked by a limb or badly hurt and carried the smell of blood on them. I do not need telling twice.

I will also give some of you city folk warning, never swim in a dam that has a broad leaf weed growing in it. Believe me, it will drown you and I don't mind how much a powerful swimmer you may believe you are. In those early days I really could swim but it beat me.

On this Sunday morning I grabbed the old twelve gauge *Harrington and Ritchenton* and headed for the big dam where there were always plenty of big fat black ducks. I would sneak-up behind the bank and wait until the ducks took to flight, up they went and I got two. One landed on the bank and the other about twelve foot out in the water.

I stripped off and went in, but it was only a few feet before the weeds started to wrap themselves around me. The more I struggled the more they wrapped around and I knew that I had not a chance. I was in about eight feet of water and it was just my good luck that there was a big tea-tree growing on the bank. A limb had grown out above the water by about two feet and I managed to grab hold of it with one hand and rip the weeds with the other. That day I left the duck for the eels and now I know not to swim in weed such as that.

Some year later we were share farming out at Bunyah and it was surely a *"Dad and Dave"* job. Even the dingoes would chase the dog up on the verandah.

Les was old enough to run the cream the two miles out to the road in he sulky and we had a nice little mare that could really get up a trot. Well he sure did some record trips and on one trip he saw some baby wild ducks in the waterhole, which was only about the size of a big kitchen table. It took quite a time to catch a couple and we gave them to the hen with chickens for her to rear.

It was the funniest thing to watch when they got down to the dam. The hen would walk out up to her chest in the water clucking, trying to coax them out. When these ducks grew up we ended up with fifteen very domesticated ducks and they were always found over with the fowl.

FLYING HIGH

One of my very favourite pastimes with the kids was catching bees off the clover. If you were quick enough and knew just the right place to hold them it was simple. I have forgotten how many times Les has been stung before *giving-it-away*. The bees would water at the hole just below the house and I would use an old Aboriginal trick. I would catch one and tie a piece of white cotton to one of its legs and then let it go to fly straight to the nest.

These bees are easy to follow on a clear sunny day and this bee, on this particular day, went straight to the nest, which was in a hollow limb up in a big old dry tree. Having found the nest we dressed ourselves up like space men. We had more armour on than any old English Knight, this after we had fell the tree of course which took us the better part of half the day.

We had no smoker to dull their fury and they attacked us on sight. They got down our boots, under the mosquito nets and up our trouser legs but with much torture and many lumps we got about a bucket full of cone, of which half was brood and so we ended up with about two cups of honey. Mum said that the next time we want honey we will spend a few shillings.

I thought about the design of hang-gliders around twenty years before they were popular. You see, as a kid I was a pro' kite flier. I once made this huge monster from big bamboo sticks and fencing wire, then layered it with paper and pasted a sheet of hessian over the whole. My idea was to get the monster in the air and then slip a rope from the tail under my arms. I figured that I could pull myself down again when I needed to.

That night I anchored this monster to the fence and the next morning when I woke I noted that I had joyfully come-up a heavy wind. However when I got out at last to check on my glider this wind had got under the glider and lifted it. It had also lifted the fence and pulled the post half out, dropping the rails. It had wrecked my lovely creation so my flying days were over for the present but in a few weeks there was going to be a flying pageant at the Old Bar and all the mighty planes in Australia were going to be there.

Smithy (Sir Charles Kingsford Smith) did not turn up but Captain Taylor (Captain Patrick Gordon Taylor) arrived with his four-seater plane and about twenty *Tiger Moths* were also there. One special plane caught my eye; it was the old *Clem Swallow*, which flew for many years after this day at Newcastle.

It was really a big two seater with a small engine and it could land against the wind at about ten glider-miles an hour and take off in not much over fifty yards. It cruised at about fifty miles per hour.

After I had calculated my own genius flying knowledge and had drank about a bottle of Inverlead Port, I was game enough to take the front seat which cost me one hard earned pound. Now I was wearing the latest headgear, a mauve cap and I looked quite lovely.

After we got about three hundred feet up into the air, I found that I was pleased that I was a bit constipated at the time. It all looked a bit far to fall and I learnt a valuable lesson; that is that you don't fly on an even-keel. You see the bumps were not all that bad but when she started to drop a few feet I confess that I did not feel quite myself.

However, after we had circled Taree and we were coming in to meet *Mother Earth* again I shoved my skull outside to see where we were about to land. Off comes my lovely cap and the pilot made a grab to rescue it but missed. We circled and watched it loop the loop, dive back flips and the like until it landed in some scrub which was so thick that a dog would not have got his jaws open to bark.

Well, later me and around twenty other *blokes* searched for that cap for about an hour as I had offered ten bob to anyone who could find it. But I'm sorry to say that it may still be somewhere around that bar yet.

JUST FAT AND CUDDLY

There's Aunty, just out of bed, looking a little glum and gloomy,
but I tell you mate, she's put on weight as her frocks ain't nice and roomy.
I'll send her west where there ain't no pests, where frogs all croak for water,
and I tell you mate she'll loose the weight and once again she'll be a corker.
I'm now heading back to my mountain shack, this only if I get the time,
for things won't go well, she'll give me hell, when she reads this little rhyme.

THE BIG FISHING BUSINESS

After the scrap iron business went bad for the country the Government pulled up with a jerk at the astonishing realization that the *Japs* were now pelting our own iron back at us. Some wise old gent in Dyers suggested that we start a fishing business.

Now, I then had a baby brother about fourteen years of age who was always looking for bargains. He was getting driving lessons on the cheap and reckoned that it was a great idea, this fishing business. In all of Krambach, Nabiac and not counting Dyers where the population was six couples and their respective dogs, we figured that we could do well. By the end of my brother's calculations I could almost see myself going to the Bank each Friday with a loaded change-bag.

Now I knew as much about fishing as diamond mining, which to say wasn't a great deal but we took ourselves off to Taree where there is a big sports store which sells self winding fishing reels and war rifles from the Bore War. You name it, they seemed to sell it.

I got down to telling this storekeeper of my big intentions and he says. *"Now Sir, it's a wonder that someone has not thought of this before, you could really do well out there and I have all the right gear so just tell me what you require."*

Well I said, *"I think I will leave that up to you,"* and he asks how much money I have to spend.

I had ten pounds, so I hauls it out to show him and began counting it out. He says, *"Now you have to have a license, that's five bob (shillings) and after that I'll see what I can do."*

At this point I was wondering if I would have enough petrol to get me home but I decide that I will run the risk. The storekeeper bought out some net, which had holes in it big enough to snare a twelve-month steer and then some rope by the half mile. Then he said that I needed some corks and fortunately he had them, as big as dinner plates they were. And I needed some lead and it took the two of us to get it all up onto the truck.

Well I says, *"What is the next performance?"*

"You have to tan that net." He says.

"What?" I answers. *"How much boot polish is that going to take?"*

"No." He answers. *"Iron bark, or wattle bark."* So he then gave me the real *low-down* on how it was all done.

Now I then jumps aboard the 'flying-bedstead' (my truck) and headed for home, wondering what I was going to do with all the cash I was about to make, perhaps a snapper boat? When I got as far as the police station I stops to go in to get my license and tells him of my big intentions.

Being a good ma the policeman advises to be sure to call every Friday as he thinks that the Sisters and Father Oregan will be sure to be good customers as well.

When I got home I grabbed the axe, as there was a big iron bark tree growing down near Gran's. After I had almost ring-barked it, Gran told me that I had enough bark there to tan a full sized bullock hide and by the time that I would get all of it into the old iron boiler with the water, then how was I going to get the net in?

It was a good question, so I left half of the bark and I got that old boiler up on the stand. Gran had only a gallon bucket and I had to climb up a steep bank from the duck pond to fill the bucket and boiler. It took a lot of time and effort.

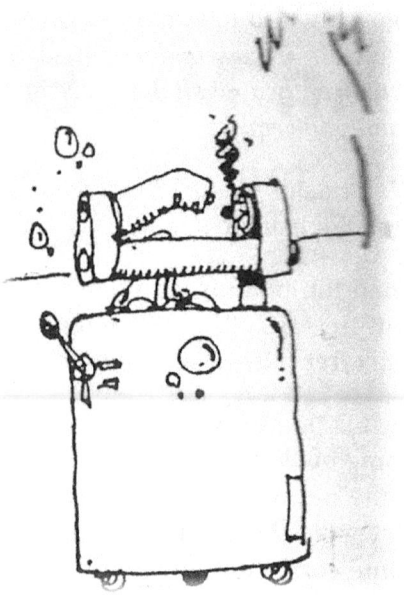

When I was ready Gran asks me what wood I intended to use. I was not invited to use hers so off I go in the twilight with no diner and no supper, to fetch the wood and at last I have a lovely roaring fire.

We bundles the net into the boiler and Gran spent much time poking it all under the water with an old broom handle which she had kept for the last twenty years. After about two hours and after I had topped the boiler up several times, Gran figured that the process should have been done by now. So in the light of the lantern we heaved and stretched that net all over the clothes-line.

The next morning it was the big cork and lead job. So we sought the local bullocky drivers knowledge and had the huge net corded and enough lead aboard to sink the Sydney Harbour ferry. After counting my expenses and deducting the price of more petrol, I had the sum of fifteen shillings. It was now time for a boat there was only one thing left to do, that was to build one for fifteen shillings.

Fired with the help of my goggled eyed brother and with a grin half way around his neck we jumped aboard the *leaping learner* (my truck) and headed for the butter factory. First we must have an anchor rope; that was easy. We got around one hundred yards of rope along with bags to put the fish in.

I then grabbed enough box nails to build a paling fence to Taree, and took off for the store. After telling the store keeper that I would be able to supply him with fish for the next six months he let us loose in his paddock of packing cases. It took us two loads and we were ready for the big fishing business.

We gulped down dinner in record time and I went off looking for the knowledge on how to build a boat. I was lucky this time as I was put onto an old retired shipwright in Nabiac. After I had told him all about my big intentions he grinned, coughed and refilled his pipe then scratched his head. By the time we had finished it was nearly dark and it concerned me that some times the light on the *flying bedstead* didn't work, so it was with some trepidation that I headed home. However this was my lucky day and I made it without incident.

By now I was as tired as a horse that had been ridden to *Bourke and back*. Yes, and all I had to do was to build a slide and this was right up my alley. Nail three boards for seats and strength and then just board up the rest. You had to be sure to put a strip of bag between each board for when the wood would swell up, it was then as water tight as a drum. It took two gum poles for the oars and these had to have a plank of board nailed to the end. These were held by two number eight fencing wire rollicks. By the time this mighty ship was ready for launching it was dark and by now everyone was fish hungry.

Next morning my grinning brother was up even before the fowls and after a lot of grunting and swearing we got half of that mighty boat up onto the *flying bedstead*, me terror of a vehicle. While one half fitted onto the back, the other half of the boat hung over the tray. We tied her down with the hundred yard of anchor rope and all was secure.

Now it was winter and the frost lay about a foot thick on the ground. To get the *flying bedstead* started we needed to jack up one wheel and after taking many turns and getting up much sweat at the crank handle, she finally fired.

It took about ten minutes before there was a big cloud of steam, which blocked out the headlights and we knew that the ice in the engine had started to melt. It wasn't long after then that we arrived at Nabiac Crossing.

At Nabiac Crossing there is a bridge there today, but then it was only known as Nabiac Crossing. To cut this long story short we got the mighty craft into the water, this after much manoeuvring. It was lucky that I pulled out all the gear first as when she hit the water; the river dropped around two feet. It all flew through the cracks and we quickly had to race our mighty craft along the bank to shallow water where she was left for an hour to allow the timbers to swell.

By now we were both a slight shade of blue as it was so cold and as the *flying bedstead* had no hood nor curtains we decided to light a bonfire and the one we lit could be seen from Nabiac.

There was plenty of driftwood and we packed it on. An old *bloke* who was getting his cows in, stopped and just gapped. I reminded him that it was a very cold day and he agreed and then marched off.

By now the sun was peeping over the prairie and we decided that the mighty craft had swollen enough, so we started to bail her out. When we had only about an ankle depth of water in the bottom of our mighty craft we took her out and strung the net across the river, anchoring it to a stump on one side and a tree on the other and then we took her back into the shallow water. There wasn't a great deal of the gunwale above the water by the time we made the shallows and we were pleased to be ashore again.

After stoking up the fire and settling to eat two corn beef sandwiches which mum had given us, we set about to wait. Now I should mention that I had been informed that when the net was ready for unloading of its catch, depending on its weight, the corks would bob up and down. If they sank you had a shark, so you had to be-ware.

We sat and we sat, until the sun was almost overhead and at last two of the corks started to bob. By now I had had fishing. We set about to bail out the *butter box ferry* (our boat) and started to haul in the net.

Funny boy, me brother, was supposed to stop the *butter box ferry* from running over the net while I stood at the back hauling it in. When he gave one big heave of the oars I landed headfirst in the drink on top of the net and I came up like an irate drowned rat.

He was laughing like a demented hyaena and for all our trouble we got ourselves two large mullet. We shipped so much water that the *butter box ferry* just made it to the shore and by then I was truly disgusted. I was wet, hungry and really cranky, particularly at the hyaena, so I flattened him and he knew it all then.

A couple of kids came along not long after and I said, *"Son would you like a boat?"* His eyes sparkled like a ten-pound diamond and I said... *"Yes, she is yours."*

I have never seen a happier pair of kids as those two. We loaded the net and other bits and pieces onto the *flying bedstead* and headed off for home. For months after people were asking me how the fishing was going but I only grinned. I got three pound from another mug for the net but for me, my fishing business had a short and glorious run before it had come to its inglorious end. I don't think I would ever make a good professional fisherman.

Nulla Nulla — Cecil R. Mackaway

THE OLD SLAB SHACK

Give me back my old slab shack out where the ironbark grow,
where the dingoes call as the shadows fall like they did so long ago.
Sitting there beside the fire while the billy's on the boil,
you soon forget your aching limbs from the strain of a hard day's toil.

As you sit there dreaming of the love ones left at home,
a night owl calls from the mountain oak, you feel so much alone.
Hear the tinkle of the hobble chain, it's the pony off down the track,
heading off towards a water hole, though I know he'll be coming back.

He'll hang around the campfire until I am ready for bed,
then he'll whinny softly for a lip-a-sugar, or perhaps that slice of bread.
A big full moon is rising behind the mountain crest,
then the bush will come to life, that's the time I love the best.

The blue gums down by the creek, that is where the gliders play,
as they fly from tree to tree you can see them plain as day.
The fireflies out in the scrub, they make a pretty sight,
like glowing sparks from a blacksmith's fire they light up the bush at night.

The possum from the tallest tree gives out his mating call,
you can hear him through the timber that grows so straight and tall.
Now the moon has risen high, it's time to go to bed,
it's just two bags between two poles and a pillow for my head.

This is my story of the bush where I'll never work again,
no more to see the firefly, or hear the hobble chain.
I'll have to stay contented, till the good Lord calls me, come.
Yet in my finest memories the bush will be my home.

THE I'S GET IT

It was a nice sunny afternoon so I grabs the old twelve gauge. I reckoned I'd have a nice baked dinner on the table, a nice big fat bunny for the kids. But after I had seen the back end of a couple-a-dozen bunnies I began to think that there is something wrong with my pretty brown eyes.

I see's this beauty in the ferns so I let him have it and with a grin like a oversexed cat I races over to collect him. To my horror, instead of bits of fur scattered around there was bits of bark and splinters everywhere. A little stump had copped the lot and now I was sure my *peepers* needed attention. It really was my *winkers* that was the problem!

After a casual walk over the ridge I fumbles me way up the alley to the eye vet. I plonks me bum down on his nice big leather chair and says; *"Mate, I think me winkers need attention."*

He gives me a look like a *stunned goanna* and then he starts to chant like the *Jew's at the Wailing Wall* as he clamps one lens after another over my blind eye.

"How's that? Is it better? Can you read the small print?"

After about twenty minutes I was beginning to get the feeling one gets after devouring a packet of epson salts, this followed up with two cups of red-hot tea.

I said. *"Mate, I'm having trouble trying to see the bloody wall!"* I don't think he liked the tone of my voice.

He grabs a telescope and fits it to one eye, an with the band around his head looked so tight I thought I would cut off the blood flow to his brain box. Then he comes over and gets me in a headlock like a Japanese bull-fighter, made me screw me eyes in every angel of the compass and then some that are not on the compass, all the time gazing into my two pretty brown eyes like a love sick cow.

After about another twenty minutes of this torture he lets out a grunt like some bloke that had been kicked below the belt by a horse. He takes three quick steps back, looks me in the blind eye and says. *"Sir,"* He called me Sir. *"Sir, ye have a cataract there as big as a horse rug."*

Well after me heart got back to its normal beat, three short and one long, I says very firmly: *"Now what's the drill?"*

He gives me another queer look like a ferret would, looking up a rabbit burrow and says; *"They will give you a local..."* I said I had had them before and after they hit you with the crowbar you don't know whether you are a local from Bourke...! *"...Then they cut a hole in your forehead and insert a finger, push the eyeball to the outside, polish it off with a clean chamois. Then if you cannot see in three hours you are blind."*

I thanked him kindly, gave him a short bow and then shot out of his den like a tomcat with his tail on fire.

I was just waiting then, to see the witch doctor down at Port (Port Macquarie, NSW) in about three weeks when I get the message that all is ready for the big op'.

Well the dentures started to rattle a bit at the thought of getting a hole punched into ones forehead and a big finger inserted to poke your eyeball out. It wasn't like just collecting first prize in the Lotto.

With Des at the wheel of my old commodore, the four of us, my Mum, Dad, Des and I, headed for the fray. Well my first encounter was with a lovely big fat *sheila* who was forty with more black paint around her *peeper's* than a Parramatta forward and two great eardrops that flapped around like loose sheets of iron in a windstorm. She led me into a room fitted with some of the most weirdest machines of torture I had ever encountered.

She got me in one of these contraptions which looked like a hippy's cow-bail, then she started the big eye game once more, with me eyelashes mixed up with me eyebrows. Next a big search light into one eye comes on and the business stared all over again.

She says: *"Sir,"* she called me Sir. *"... Sir, please look at my left ear."*

Now that took a bit of doing, her ears seemed to flap every time she took a breath. Then I had to look at the other big eardrop and then up, then down, with this big five hundred-candle power searchlight piercing my poor little birdbrain for ten minutes.

By now I'm seeing stars that I never knew existed, then she grabs me by the arm and leads me to another semi-dark room to meet the witch doctor, the one that was going to punch that window in my forehead.

He gave me a stare, up and down like he was about to part with around ten thousand dollars for a prize bull. Then he gets me head stuck in another vet machine, one I'm sure he had bought second-hand from Hitler.

This time the searchlight was so strong that it singed me eyebrows. Well after ten minutes of this torture he tells me to look at the ceiling, then he hits me in both eyes with half a cup of eye mixture, smelling of spirits of salts and stale whisky. Well I flew into the air like a kangaroo that had just received a bum-full of buckshot, jumped around the room on one leg and then the other and now I am as blind as a bat!

I heard a voice come out of the dark saying; *"Come back in six months and then we will operate, in the meantime we will lend you a stronger lens."*

That fat lady took over and I know it was her, I could hear her eardrops bumping her shoulder pads. She leads me out to the debt collector and this is where Mum came into the circus, or Belsen torture camp, not sure which is the better description.

"How much?" she says.

A shaky voice behind the counter replied. *"Sixty dollars please."* And I heard mum grind her fangs.

"How much do I get back? Half! If Bob Hawke is still in the land of the living." She dives her hand into the big bookmakers bag, the one with the reinforced shoulder strap, dodging the death adder and the rabbit trap and paid-up. Then she puts back a roll as big as a two-gallon milk bucket.

After I gets' home, I gets me eyeballs *inter'* a big bucket of water, coming up for air every five minutes. These days my eyes are much better, I can even see the time on the old grandfather's clock and I thank the Gods that I'm not need to go to the eye vets again... yet!

THE HIPPY AND THE RABBIT TRAP

Some hippies from the city got sick of smog and strife,
so they came up to the country to lead a happy life.
They bought some gumtree country along up at Taylors Arm,
where they could grow their grass, right away from any harm.

Tucker was getting short this day and this Hippy getting thinner,
so he thought he'd catch a rabbit an' have himself a dinner.
He went up to the farmer who was a decent chap,
he lends the Hippy a nice sharp hoe along with a rabbit trap.

After he walked along for a mile or two his feet were getting sore,
luck was really running with him, he was right at the bunnies door.
Bunny was down there right beneath him as he had his morning nap,
Ne'r dreaming there's a Hippy up above him with a trap.

The Hippy was a scholar and he hadn't the slightest doubt,
that anything that went right in must surely come right out.
So he started digging, work he'd never done before,
he dug a nice clean hole right there at the bunnies door.

Then he began to set the trap, well everything went wrong,
that nasty trap gave an awful snap and grabbed his poor wing-wong.
He gave one awful scream, like a curlew in the night,
them goannas that were all about went for trees like emu's off in fright.

He yelled and bucked in pain, the bush ringing with his screams,
his shorts of many colours were now stretching at the seams.
That trap held on like a bulldogs bite and there was nuthin' he could do,
so he headed for the farmhouse. Boy how that Hippy flew!

The farmers wife was getting dinner like most all good housewives do,
when she though she heard the cry of the poor lonely grey curlew.
She peeped out through the window and then did she get a fright,
for never in all her life did she see such an awful sight.

She felt sorry for being a peeper, for pelting down that hill,
there came a loony streaker that couldn't at all keep still.
She let out one awful scream and left the kitchen in full flight,
heading out toward her hubby screaming at him of her plight.

Hearing her story as it unfolded, he gathered up his wits,
he jumped aboard his trusty Holden, thinking how these Hippies are all twits
He found that dirty Hippy, 'e was all astride a log,
his face was white as paste, his eyes swollen like a frog.

When he seen his trouble he made him lay right down,
he released him with a hobnailed boot, an' they flattened out for town.
When the nurses had seen his trouble they all began to grin,
by this time it all had swollen up to the size of a treacle tin.

They packed him up in ice or cold and nice to help the thing lay down,
while the farmer in his Holden headed back out of that old country town.
After some weeks had passed and no hippy had come in sight,
the farmer went to see the quack about the hippies' plight.

He said that Hippy,
yes... he's doing pretty fine,
but I fear poor Hippies future,
it's ruined for quite some time.

NULLA'S THANKS

Old Nulla's gone all gypsy an his ears are rather long,
an while the Missus cooks the chook he sings a gypsy song.
About them distant ranges where the roos and wombats roam,
an about his friend and loved ones he has left back here at home.
Yes this is my homeland where the gums and wattle grow,
and for a while you'll find me where the Murrumbidgee flows.

At night beside the campfire where the stars shine clear and bright,
you may hear the call o'night, an birds that pass o'head in flight.
I'm an Australian Bushman and no matter where I roam,
in the bush or on the river to me it's always home.
So now you know the reason why I sing this gypsy song,
I'm heading for my bushland the place where I belong.
So we thank all you kind people for all that you have done,
and in the pages of our diary there's the name of every one.

Old Nulla Mack

THE BIG POP

In a place called Wombat Creek there's church people by the score,
you'll find them on a Sunday morn' around the old church door.
They talk about their best test cows and sell a pig or two,
or perhaps a mob of bullocks before the mornings through.

At last the preacher comes along an' has a world or two,
with his hair all combed atop his head like a crested cockatoo.
He's got a dial 'ard as a shovel, an' he's as poor as a half starved crow,
he reminds me a lot of somethin' they embalmed in pyramids long ago.

When the bell begins to ring they shove thumbs right in their ears,
while thinking of the thirst they'll have for Mrs Murphy's beers.
There's that big sheila by the window, she had a breakfast of onion soup,
every time she got the pain down her back, it seemed to make her stoop.

While the preacher rambled on, about the sin he saw in man,
the strings in her boned corset, were getting tight as a rubber band.
Just then the preacher stopped his yodel an' the organ made a start,
that is where the onion gas, an' the big sheila had to part.

She slightly rose up off her seat with both heels hard on the floor,
as her eyeballs seemed to meet, it was like a canon roar.
It drowned out the old church organ and stopped the church wall clock.
That alter swayed as the parson prayed, it went off with such a pop.

Everything went silent! None was game to breathe,
until they all ran short of breath then they thought it time to leave.
Some flew out the windows, some headed for the door.
As the parson removed his glasses, for the first time he really swore.

There stood the plate quite empty and no one seemed to care,
whether he lived on damper, or lived on good fresh air.
Everything looked rosy as the sun shone clear and bright,
while Mrs Murphy down at the pub rubbed her hands in sheer delight.

The big sheila with the corset had made the air go blue.
The preacher cursed all onions in Ireland, an' on up to Queensland too.
Mrs Murphy with big sad eyes, said sure ain't it a shame,
to think you had to kneel in church while feeling so much a pain.

So that's the way of country life,
in the place where I was born.
That's where I'd like to be once more,
out among the oats and corn.

MY FAREWELL SPEECH

One Nulla's gone a fishing ten miles up Wombat Creek,
where the wattle blooms in springtime and the air is fresh and sweet.
No more he'll climb those long steel steps nor curse that big phone bell,
but no matter where I wander whether the road be flat or steep,
I will always have this place to thank for putting me on Easy Street.
So to all of you that's present and to those that's passed away,
I have a thought in my heart for each of you today.
So let this be my farewell speech and I hope to make it clear,
I have found you all the best of mates, both honest and sincere.

By Nulla Nulla
No school, no scholar. I was always known as Nulla Nulla.

A NOTE FROM THE AUTHOR
CECIL ROY MACKAWAY

Nulla Nulla is a stick, with a great knob on one end. One of its uses is when a young Aboriginal lad was beginning to feel a bit lonely and he reckoned he needed a wife, he would wait until the middle of the day when it was a bit hot and he would sneak up to the water hole where all the young girls from other tribes would be having a swim. He would pick the best and spring on her like greyhound with a bull-ant under his tail and if she gave any trouble he gave her a slight tap on the noggin with his *nulla*, throw her over his shoulder and head back to his tribe. In this way they were married.

AROUND THE CAMPFIRE

A travelogue series and other tales on Australia.
Stories from Around the Campfire

The 'Around the Campfire' series is a collection of the tales by writer Jan Hawkins and others, collected as she travels around Australia. The stories are not meant to advertise but are more a collection of anecdotes and recounts of the treasures and tales that can be heard and found on this  unique island Continent that is Australia. Many are travelogues, some a tales by others but they all bring to the reader a unique Australian character.

Visit http://oldiesatlarge.com.au and discover other adventures to be had around the vast continent, Australia

For Publications in E-book and Print

janhawkins.com.au

www.ingramcontent.com/pod-product-compliance
Lightning Source LLC
Chambersburg PA
CBHW071749040426
42446CB00012B/2504